ANTE-BELLUM HOUSES OF

Natchez

By J. Wesley Cooper

Foreword By
Beverly Warner Martin, A.I.A.

Floor Plans By
Edna Elizabeth Farmer
and
James Harmond Arnold

SOUTHERN HISTORICAL PUBLICATIONS, INC.

Natchez, Mississippi

1983

Printed by

HEDERMAN BROTHERS

Jackson, Mississippi

U.S.A.

Dedicated to

My Daughters, Carolyn and Deborah,

who have brought so much happiness

into my life.

ACKNOWLEDGMENTS

My gratitude to my many friends and the organizations who cooperated with me in compiling this book.

MR. F. R. BLANKENSTEIN, for the use of his collection of old photographs
MRS. MARTIN NATHANSON, assistance in compiling the text for this book
MR. AND MRS. GEORGE T. SMITH, for their encouragement and photographic assistance
MR. FRANK PARSONS, supervising the drawing of floor plans and the use of old photographs
THE STAFF OF HEDERMAN BROTHERS
RICHARD W. SMITH, account representative, Hederman Brothers
MR. AND MRS. REGINALD L. WALSH, encouragement
MISS EDNA ELIZABETH FARMER, drawing floor plans
MR. JAMES HARMOND ARNOLD, drawing floor plans
MISS MARY POSTLETHWAITE, researching Spanish records
MR. AND MRS. FRANCIS GEDDES, for the use of an old photograph
MRS. HARRY DAWES, correction and editing
MRS. SUE MARIE WILLIAMS, typing
MRS. J. ARTHUR EIDT, typing
MR. AND MRS. CLARENCE EYRICH, JR.
MISS JEANERETTE HARLOW, for the use of old photographs and encouragement
MR. AND MRS. SAUL HABAS, encouragement
MR. J. EARL LE BOUEF, photographic printing and processing
MRS. J. WESLEY COOPER, my wife, for her understanding and patience and immense help in editing material.
MR. GEORGE EYRICH
MRS. ESTELLE COOPER, my mother, whose encouragement has meant so much
MR. ERASTUS BUSH
MR. JOSEPH ZUCCARO
MR. GEORGE NOSSER
MR. BEVERLY WARNER MARTIN, for his excellent description of architectural styles and the writing of the Foreword
MR. B. HAMMOND DAVIDSON
MR. AND MRS. AUSTIN LEFTWICH
MR. JOE DI STEFANO
MISS ELENORA GRALOW
MISS ANN MacNEIL
DR. AND MRS. JAMES SAVOY, encouragement
MR. WILLIAM S. BURNS
MR. PAUL SHILLING
MR. MALCOLM D. RAWORTH, JR.
MRS. JOSEPH B. KELLOGG
MR. AND MRS. HYDE D. JENKINS
THE MORRISON FAMILY AT GLOUCESTER
THE PILGRIMAGE GARDEN CLUB
MISS AUDRY SHIELDS, typing
DR. AND MRS. HOMER WHITTINGTON
MRS. R. A. W. BELTZHOOVER

MR. AND MRS. CHARLES EVERETTE RATCLIFFE
MRS. LAURIE RATCLIFF
MRS. EDNA HOWARD
MR. AND MRS. J. BALFOUR MILLER
MR. AND MRS. N. L. CARPENTER
MR. McVEY BUTLER
MR. AND MRS. RICHARD DURKIN
MRS. GEORGE M. D. KELLY
MR. AND MRS. CHARLES J. BYRNE
MR. AND MRS. EARL HART MILLER
MRS. DOUGLAS H. MacNEIL
MRS. MARY LAMBERT
MR. AND MRS. J. FERD SESSIONS
MR. AND MRS. RICHARD A. CAMPBELL
MR. S. H. LAMBDIN
MRS. ANNE VAUGHN
MRS. W. A. HENDRIX
MR. AND MRS. JOHN SMITH
MR. AND MRS. TOM L. KETCHINGS
THE NATCHEZ GARDEN CLUB
MRS. ELLEN GOODELL
MR. AND MRS. LUCIEN GUIN, SR.
MR. S. BARNETT SERIO
MR. AND MRS. LAWRENCE ADAMS
MR. AND MRS. T. B. BUCKLES, SR.
MR. AND MRS. T. B. BUCKLES, JR.
MR. AND MRS. GEORGE M. MARSHALL
MRS. SINGLETON GARDNER
THE CHARISIMA CORPORATION
THE MARSHALL FAMILY AT RICHMOND
MRS. H. W. NUGENT
DAUGHTERS OF THE AMERICAN REVOLUTION
MR. AND MRS. ORRICK METCALFE
THE COLONIAL DAMES OF AMERICA
MR. AND MRS. WILLIAM CARL McGEHEE
THE HONORABLE JOHN R. JUNKIN
MR. AND MRS. FRANK FAUNTLEROY
MR. AND MRS. ELLIOT TRIMBLE
THE MERRILL FAMILY AT AIRLIE
MR. AND MRS. L. A. WHITE
MR. AND MRS. HUNTER GOODRICH
MR. AND MRS. HAROLD LEISURE
DR. HAROLD C. HAWKINS AND MR. H. HAL GARNER
MRS. W. W. MAXIE
MR. JAMES H. WILLIAMS, JR.
DR. AND MRS. GEORGE MOSS
THE NATCHEZ ADAMS COUNTY CHAMBER OF COMMERCE
TRINITY EPISCOPAL DAY SCHOOL
MR. AND MRS. BAZILE R. LANNEAU

FOREWORD

Natchez is peculiarly such a place as people meet at the end of a trail down the ridge from the Appalachian mountain chain and as far up the great river as a sailing vessel of the time might conveniently come; a promontory overlooking this great stream and rich lands as far as the eye could see. One could only hope the Gates of Heaven were as well marked. So, they came and settled here and the many who are their heritage today have trouble identifying Heaven. "Is it like *Natchez?*" they innocently ask without conceit and as many unwary young gentlemen find on marrying Natchez belles, it is part of the marriage contract that they not leave here.

Particularly, in its time when great fortunes could be made from the cotton plantations, new generations of Americans were moving on the flood tide of expansion of a young new nation. This was a new era — not a revival. Those who came represented strong ties with the eastern seaboard and a large percentage were well educated — some in Europe. They brought with them their desires, cultures and ambitions. They came not as rude frontiersmen. They expected to build greatly and fashion a society unsurpassed. What happened was not accidental but something that flowered from the wealth of its people, their knowledge, their organization of slavery and equipment and goods, and except for a very few things — a complete society. It came of age and then suddenly like the Sleeping Beauty it was to become transfixed — for nearly a hundred years.

O Tempores, O Mores — Outwardly, life is as modern here as in any small southern city; as strident and cluttered as any market place. Yet, across the years the shadow of the more glorious days casts the spell on the people influencing them in a practice of gracious living, more extravagant manners and flowery speech than you are apt to encounter elsewhere. This is not to say it doesn't cover a razor sharp blade on occasion. It is real and not feigned. What one hears when welcomed is an acceptance of the stranger at the gate for what he is — a guest. Waste it not for it is genuine.

The charm of the Homes is not in their number, for that diminishes the value of a rarity, but in their infinite variety, as many as in a Paganini theme. Seldom is found something that follows strictly from the patterns of Vignola or Palladio or on down to Adam or Wren. The use of the orders is highly cavalier and some of the works are derived from other sources because the French and the Spanish left their mark here as well. Some are attributable to environmental need and best were furnished from semi-tropical experience finding its way up from the West Indies and the Caribbean. For once, everyone came from some other place.

Much is dependent on the entourage. Imagine it without the neighborhoods and atmosphere you first witnessed as an entree, the clusters of lesser dwellings, the majestic sheltering trees, the cross-cut roofs of the humble cabins and door-yard gardens and the frame is gone from the picture.

The aura of its history is not hollow but teeming with interest, with ambitions, with jealousies and bitter conflicts, humor, joy and laughter along with generous and fine instincts and occasional heroic act or venture and extraordinary enterprise. The people were vigorous and vital and sought more than the ordinary, and sought hard to achieve and to keep more than the ordinary. The customs were as they were brought from the Carolinas and Virginia and down the Great River, and from Spain, and from France and not from any frontier style, except that the wilderness had to be coped with.

Suddenly deprived of their great wealth and the means to carry on their economy and isolated by a great change in the direction of the country's movement, their way of life shrivelled into bare existence. They could no longer keep up their great homes. The Houses fell into disuse and decay. A large number were lost to fire and carelessness. The surviving ones were in more recent times restored with good judgment. A wry blessing was that some could not be changed or "improved" because the owners could not afford it. There was no great commerce to cause them to be removed. The threat even today is that the Houses and other authentic architectural examples may be pulled down or changed beyond recognition to satisfy an immediate advantage. The need for proper upkeep and preservation means and restoration is vacuous and requires a vigilance on the part of those interested. As much of this comment is meant for "the entourage" as for the great houses themselves.

As much as architects would like it to be a new building, a new center or other group modeled on the past is no more acceptable than any other type of reproduction, however fine. A partial response in some cases may be accomplished where a restoration is complete providing it be exact, on its original site and thoroughly documented. Usually what the viewer seeks is to see the original in a setting and with the proper accommodations to enable him to envision its being used as the original owner would have done.

The earliest non-Indian habitations were doubtless crude and small. Both the Spanish and the French were inclined to proceed as early as possible to more permanent types of buildings. These were apt, too, to be small and appearing "tight." One would look for timberwork in the attic space to be rugged, well pinned and having the appearance of having been done by shipwrights, if Spanish. Decoration, if any, would be tight, intricate and sharply defined viz *Connelly's Tavern.*

The French construction, somewhat more loosely mixed woodwork in their masonry and tended to use roundness and softness more in their detail. More of their column caps, stair newels and railings were rounder. Most of what we had of both were between Market Street and the river and to the South of Market Street.

The English and the Americans coming brought broader vision and more expansive ideas. Their first buildings were probably crude as well. As they began to refind beyond their first farmhouse establishments and a trend was begun toward the great houses they obscured their humbler beginnings.

Rosalie is perhaps the best example of the Southerner adapting the Georgian in the Tuscan Order with its comparatively spare use of exquisite detail inside and out, nevertheless holding true to the concept on all four elevations. Both earlier and later than it were the story-and-a-half house with its long front porch. Their development is somewhat obscure but certainly most natural and adapted to this area. One might suspect more plebian beginnings but the refinement is here.

As the wealth of the area grew the Homes and the styles changed and became more ostentatious, larger and the Ionic and Corinthian Orders were more widely used with profuse ornamentation, though sometimes fronts and other elevations differed as at *Arlington* and *Melrose.* Somewhere in between came a different expression that was called the Greek Revival influence that is recalled in *Green Leaves,* and *D'Evereux,* that is sharp, crisp and reserved in detail, design and discipline. One can not say this period fell just in certain years, only after 1820.

Some, such as *Richmond* or *Hope Farm,* underwent two or three expansions in different architectural periods. Many did this unsuccessfully and are not worthy of note. In the lush but cloudy years just before the Civil War, the largest and most extravagant were built and every care and luxury of the time was lavished on them. Most of these were very formal. These are admired and marvelled and justly so, but the greatest feeling of intimacy and appeal for many comes in something they can take away. The impression of those rambling structures such as *Linden* or *The Elms* that are so beautifully scaled to the human need with the exquisite detail of *Linden* or the surprise features of *The Elms* is proved in their great attraction and dissolving of reservations. Interesting too is the successful handling of a difficult situation that all of us have seen fail so many times — a rather formal comparatively small building on a high corner. The formality even heightens inside. It is not "put on."

There is never a stopping place. But if there is, let's call it here. Next time, try to make up your mind what it is you most want to see and take the time to study it in detail and in full enjoyment.

That you can take with you.

BEVERLY WARNER MARTIN, A.I.A.

TABLE OF CONTENTS

SPECIAL ILLUSTRATIONS

PROLOGUE

. . . . It is just a small city, *Natchez*, much smaller than its fame would have one believe. It sits on its high bluff overlooking the Mississippi River, and across the river lie the fertile Louisiana lowlands which helped to shape the destiny of *Natchez*. It is a city that lived . . . and flourished . . . then suddenly declined for many years until its progress began again. This had to be so that the ante-bellum houses which *Natchez* possesses could be saved for posterity.

Natchez with its scores of ante-bellum houses — the largest concentration of magnificent mansions anywhere in the United States. Why are they here? Because at one time, more than a century ago, *Natchez* was the center of prosperity of the entire South, and prosperous planters built these houses. Then circumstances changed, and the descendants of these planters came upon hard times. They could not change with the years, they could not modernize, they had to live in what had become shabby grandeur. The sturdily built mansions endured, defying the ravages of time, until a new generation could discover and restore them, and throw them open for the world to see.

The destiny of *Natchez* began when Bienville, the French explorer and colonizer, arrived in 1716 to establish on the high bluffs Fort Rosalie to strengthen France's claims to the entire region from the Great Lakes to the Gulf of Mexico.

But perhaps *Natchez's* destiny was set thousands of years before in the pattern of the earth when the great stoneless bluffs were thrown up on the east bank of the Mississippi River, and the swampy flatlands developed on the west. For every man who viewed those bluffs from the very first Indian down through the explorers and settlers must have been struck by the thought that here Nature had built a natural site for a settlement — high enough to escape the mightiest floods of the Mississippi, fertile enough to produce abundant crops, situated to serve as a lookout for enemies approaching on the river.

It was left to Bienville with a handful of men, in 1716, to build the fort which was ill-fated for the French. Not far from the fort lived the *Natchez* Indians, a tribe of Sun-Worshipers whose numbers were in the thousands. Thirteen years after the fort was founded occurred the Great Massacre of *Natchez*, in which many of the early French colonists died at the hands of the Indians. The fort was abandoned by the French, and once again the Indians were the only inhabitants of the yellow bluffs.

Thirty-five years passed, and in the summer of 1764, down the Mississippi came a war vessel bearing the British flag. On the bluffs of *Natchez*, on the site of Fort Rosalie, British troops took over the garrison under the protection of the warship and a new name was given — Fort Panmure. But the bluffs were not destined to remain long in British hands. The American Revolution came, followed by the creation of the United States of America. The British were losing their hold in the New World; and Spain took over, sending a Spanish commandant to the post of *Natchez* in 1781.

Meanwhile, during these years, the land of the bluffs began to be settled — first by a trickle of the hardy, then more and more others found their way to the fertile farm lands. By the time the Spaniards yielded to the United States, and the American flag was raised over the garrison in 1797, *Natchez* was a sizable community. And when Mississippi became a state in 1817, *Natchez* was thriving.

This was only a little more than 170 years ago. In a man's lifetime, primitive wilderness had become a bustling town. The Natchez District at that time was not just a settlement on the bluffs. It ran from the mouth of the Yazoo River on the North to Bayou Sara on the South, and was estimated at over two million acres.

In all this vast territory lived the men who were destined to become a group known even now in *Natchez*, as "the old planters." These men and their children were the ones who built the mansions in the wilderness. You might term them the lavish pioneers.

Who were these people? How did they arrive in the wilderness?

Some of them were of British nobility — younger sons without inheritances. Some were of French descent, others Spanish or Portuguese. Each nationality left its adventurous sons as the nations moved in and moved out.

The majority of them combined an Old World polish and education with a New World spirit. Some were of the middle-class, without background or education, but with natural qualities suited to advancement in an uncut land.

During their early years, when indigo was one of the main crops of this area, there was little hint of the magnificent structures that were to come. About the time that the United States took over, just before the turn of the nineteenth century, a visitor wrote that the homes in the *Natchez* district were very plain, that the furniture was nailed together. The visitor wrote that some of the houses were neat, but even among persons of consequence they were not elaborately furnished.

But by 1835, a great change had been wrought. *Natchez* was incorporated as a town on April 9, 1803 under Governor Claiborne, and those thirty years saw the advent of cotton as a crop, and tremendous prosperity. A traveler visiting in 1835 wrote that there was as much style and fine dressing as in Philadelphia, and certainly more than in New Orleans. As money flowed into the hands of the planters, they began to turn to outward display, perhaps to vie with one another in the fineness of their homes.

Using slave labor and oftentimes native clay for bricks, they erected structures that took months and years to build. Many kinds of architecture were employed, as we shall see from the photographs produced in this book. Often the planters combined memories of childhood homes with adaptations to the new land in which they lived. Successive generations, adding a wing or two, sometimes did so without regard for the architecture of the main house. Yet the overall effect has a charm that is a large part of the charm of *Natchez*.

The general trend of the architecture of the houses follows a specific pattern which ties in with the history of the land. For instance, the earliest settlers were not much concerned with embellishments, but were very much concerned with getting stout walls around themselves and their families as protection against marauders of the wilderness. Some of these early houses have endured — not because they were built to last long past a century, but because they were built as strong as the settlers knew how to make them to serve as personal fortifications.

These houses have thick walls of seasoned cypress put together with wooden pegs. Timbers were hand-hewn, or else were bought from owners of boats who had brought freight down the Mississippi River, and were unable to travel up the river against the current. These boats, having served their purpose, were demolished, and the timbers sold for house material.

At first the settlers built low ceilings in their houses — and these low ceilings are in many of the earlier houses of *Natchez*. But as the years passed, and the pioneers endured the hot humid summers, the ceilings were raised higher and higher, until the interiors of the later houses were almost castle-like in appearance.

Then there were the galleries. The earliest houses had no galleries, but were square box-like affairs, for there was little lolling on galleries in the first days of *Natchez*. But as the years passed, and some men grew rich, they began to add their own versions of what in other parts of the world were known as porticoes. The galleries were usually spacious, made for enjoyment and to catch the play of the summer breezes. At first they were long wooden structures across the front and rear of the house. Then, as the Georgian influence came to *Natchez*, they had great columns, often majestic; and finally in the lush years they assumed the austere elegance of the Greek design.

Those were the periods of *Natchez* — the early pioneer, when men and women had little time to think of anything except the necessities of life, a period which extended into the nineteenth century; the Georgian period, which predated the lavish era because men were beginning to amass fortunes and to build mansions; and finally the lavish, or "lush" period as it is known in *Natchez*, when all the social graces were being practiced, when the polish of the well-to-do had been acquired, when the houses began to show the Greek Revival influence. This last period began about 1830, and extended to the Civil War.

Settlers came into *Natchez* by two routes — The Mississippi River and the *Natchez Trace*. Heavy freight found its way to *Natchez* by the river, and as the country grew more populous, *Natchez* became a thriving port. A settlement grew up on the land beneath *Natchez's* tall bluffs, and this settlement became the notorious *Natchez-Under-the-Hill*. Here were the wharfs where cotton was loaded, and where freight from the North was unloaded. As the steamboat era came, the port assumed tremendous proportions. Amidst all the bustling activity, were the bars and taverns which the rougher element frequented. This was a frontier town. And while the rich planters were building their beautiful mansions atop the bluffs, a rough world of its own was building itself below.

The second route into *Natchez* was the *Natchez Trace*, an old buffalo trail that became an Indian trail, and finally a much-traveled highway from Nashville, Tennessee, to *Natchez*. Down this trail came many of the pioneer families with their few possessions, braving the elements to a strange new land. Robbers plagued this route, and perhaps it is because of these pillagers that the houses were built stout enough to endure into our generation.

Since *Natchez* was the center of this part of the country, it is only natural that some of the famous people of that day found their way here — Andrew Jackson, Aaron Burr, John James Audubon, Jenny Lind. In the years when cotton was king, there was no limit to the lavish life of the *Natchez* rich.

Then in 1861 came the Civil War, and the period of Reconstruction following it. *Natchez* was exceedingly fortunate in escaping the worst ravages of the war; but one magnificent home, said to have been possibly the finest of all, Clifton, was destroyed to make way for a Union fortification.

Although the Union gunboat, Essex, fired on *Natchez* on September 2, 1862, some believe that the firing was done after some *Natchez* citizens had provoked the incident. It is said that the officers of the gunboat were seeking ice for their wounded, and were met with hostility in *Natchez*. Certainly the times were trying enough, and the hard beset residents could easily have misinterpreted the meaning of the gunboat. At any rate, a barrage of shells was fired, many hitting in all parts of *Natchez*. There was one casualty, 7-year old Rosalie Beekman. This child was the great-aunt of Mrs. Cooper, the author's wife. She was struck by a shell fragment while fleeing with her parents to what was believed to be a safer shelter.

When the Federal soldiers occupied *Natchez*, they set up headquarters in that group of houses closest to the river and to the center of town — *The Burn, Arlie* and *Rosalie* among them.

With the Civil War and Reconstruction, came the end of the lavish life in *Natchez*. The great houses needed large staffs of servants, and few owners could afford such retinues.

Some of the houses were sold, and had a succession of owners. Some of the owners, and their children, clung to the houses, and saw them fall into disrepair. In some of the houses, the exquisite furnishings were sold because the owners needed the money for necessities. Others kept their furniture though it gathered layer after layer of dust and cobwebs. One or two persons, working hard to maintain a livelihood, could not polish even the most valuable of furniture of such vast dimensions.

So the years passed and the fortunes of *Natchez* fluctuated with the times, but never returned to the lavish scale. Some families recouped some of their losses, some even became wealthy, but never in the magnitude of ante-bellum days. Meanwhile railroads were threading the South, but no main line ever passed through *Natchez*. Other cities reached the importance of *Natchez*, then passed it by — Baton Rouge to the South, Vicksburg to the North, Jackson to the East. Into the early twentieth century *Natchez* became known as the little city that could not progress.

New styles in houses were coming into vogue, new types of furniture. Many families tenaciously held on to their relics of bygone days, but just as many sold them for food, for clothing, or just to make way for modern things. In the first quarter of the twentieth century, much of the furnishings must have gone begging.

But the houses remained, hidden amidst ancient shrubbery planted by long-dead hands. They remained until 1932, when the ladies of *Natchez* inaugurated the first *Natchez Pilgrimage*, an event that has assumed international importance. The houses were scrubbed and dusted, and thrown open in a timid venture that grew to gigantic proportions. Each home-owner received a percentage of the receipts of the Pilgrimage, and with this money began the slow work of restoration of the houses and furnishings.

Then other factors began to enter the picture. Industry, looking to the South, found its way to *Natchez*. A new group of people moved in — job holders in new plants. And oil was discovered around *Natchez*, both in Mississippi and across the river in Louisiana.

A surge of life took possession of the town — the kind that was easing the South out of agricultural dependency toward other industry.

Little subdivisions have sprung up in the shadows of the mansions. Many of the owners have sold off acreage around their homes for these subdivisions that are made up of modern little ranch houses, snuggled at the feet of the mansions whose halls alone are as large as one entire modern house.

. . . Thus *Natchez* has preserved for the world a living record of the years when Cotton was King —a page in the history of America. Some of the houses have burned, or been destroyed by tornadoes or by war. But all these that are photographed in this book remain, with the exception of several — a tribute to the pioneer spirit that always must rise above the elemental things of life.

THE ELMS

1782-1856

In the heart of Natchez, only two blocks from Main Street, is one of the most unusual of all the ante-bellum homes. Enormous oaks and masses of ancient shrubbery reveal only the outlines of pink stucco, which, upon closer observation, proves to be of provocative design.

This home is called *The Elms*, although just why it is so called, and who built it, is not known. Records on the grant of land which *The Elms* occupies go back to 1782 to William Barland and it is believed that he was the builder.

Definitely the older part of *The Elms* is Spanish. It has solid brick walls plastered in pink and low ceilings. When it was built, it had galleries running all around the house. In 1856, Mr. and Mrs. David Stanton built an annex with a parlor downstairs and the master bedroom and dressing room upstairs. This annex blends beautifully into the architecture of the earlier portion. In contrast, the ceilings here are high and the bedroom is elevated from the second floor of the original house.

Part of the galleries were enclosed in the remodeling and made into an upper and lower hall. A wrought iron stairway is in the hall and is one of the most outstanding in this part of the country. This circular stairway dates from the early section of the house.

The Elms is equipped with a system of bells which ring in the servants' quarters and were known in the early days as slave bells. Each room and gallery has a bell of different pitch. Servants knew in which part of the house they were wanted by the tinkle of the bells.

The Elms is now the home of Mrs. Joseph B. Kellogg. Mrs. Kellogg is the grand-daughter of Mr. and Mrs. Moseley J. P. Drake, who moved to *The Elms* in 1868. Mr. Drake was the nephew of the Rev. Benjamin M. Drake, a renowned Methodist minister of early Natchez. Rev. Drake served from 1828 to 1832 as president of Elizabeth Female Academy, one of the famous girls' schools in Early American history.

Because of its antiquity, *The Elms* has had many prominent owners, among them being Samuel Postlethwaite, who purchased *The Elms* in 1818 and later deeded a lot to the Female Charitable Society, of which his wife was a member. On this lot the Society founded an orphanage, which was the beginning of the present Protestant Orphanage.

Many years later the Carpenter School was built on an adjoining lot where the billiard hall of *The Elms* once stood.

Originally the house was surrounded by 105 acres, but most of this land has been engulfed by city blocks. *The Elms* has retained about 3 acres. Three bricked cisterns, one of which can still be used, add to the charm of the grounds. In the spring, heavy-growing camellias, azaleas, wisteria, and bulbs form a riot of color. The summer brings gnarled crepe myrtles that burst into bright pink. With the coming of fall, the changing yellows and reds of the trees create a magnificent display, and in the winter, ancient oaks set knotted branches against the sky.

There were formerly three summer houses on the grounds. They were octagonal in shape, with every alternate panel being a doorway, and were paved with brick. Two of these have been destroyed. The remaining one was used by Mrs. Kellogg's grandmother to cage an eagle, and is now known as the "Eagle House."

The Elms' garden is one of the better known beauty spots of Natchez, because it is accessible to every passerby.

PLATE I *THE ELMS*

An afternoon in the Spring of 1870
at The Elms.
COURTESY MRS. J. B. KELLOGG

Dining room at The Elms.

The Elms — Parlor located in the annex built in 1856.

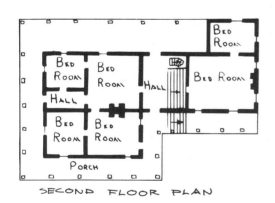

SECOND FLOOR PLAN

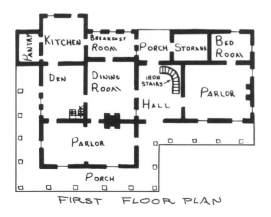

FIRST FLOOR PLAN

STANTON HALL

1851-1857

Stanton Hall, in the heart of Natchez, stands today as the finest example of the lavish culture of the South in the decade before the Civil War.

Frederick Stanton, wealthy Natchez commission merchant, began *Stanton Hall* in 1851, and planned it after his ancestral house in Ireland. It took five years to build; and while the bricks were being burned by slaves on the ground, and the walls were taking shape, Stanton was in Europe ordering the finest furnishings for this magnificent house.

A city block forms the grounds for *Stanton Hall*. A heavy iron grill fence surrounds it. It may here be noted that in later years this beautiful house is said to have been sold for less than the cost of the fence.

The house has large double galleries, with stately Grecian columns. Both upper and lower galleries have beautifully designed grillwork railings. The floor of the lower gallery is of gray and white marble, and the wide steps are granite.

The building has a tremendous hall on its lower floor, seventy-four feet long. A beautiful carved arch breaks the severity of the hall. Doorways entering other rooms from the hall have exquisite hand carvings, and rise to tremendous heights.

The whole feeling of the house is one of spaciousness. The drawing room to the right is seventy feet long. An arch here, elaborately hand carved in Italy, is of extreme interest to architect and layman because it has no support from the floor. The mantels are of Carrara marble — carved with fruits, flowers and cherubs. When *Stanton Hall* was built, the period of the black marble mantel had passed, and white marble was the vogue. The parlors open into a side grilled balcony.

To the left of the hall is the library. Behind this room, the mahogany railed stairway leads to six airy bedrooms. The forty by twenty-two foot banquet hall is beyond the stair alcove and is graced by two white marble mantels on either side of a pair of windows almost ceiling high.

The chandeliers of *Stanton Hall* create much interest for the history of Natchez they tell in figures. These figures were all made from hand-carved forms which Mr. Stanton took to France.

The builder of *Stanton Hall* died suddenly, not long after he had moved into the house. Then came the Civil War, and in the years that followed, this elegant house changed hands several times. Once it was used as a select ladies' school, Stanton College for Young Ladies. One owner tore down part of the outside wing, used as the kitchen, with bedrooms upstairs, probably because it was "too much house."

In 1940, the Pilgrimage Garden Club purchased the house, and the club has restored it to its former brilliance. It is once again the show place of Natchez, perhaps even more beautiful, because now the stately live oaks that were saplings in Stanton's day are tall and majestic, casting lacy shadows on this most elaborate of all Natchez houses.

PLATE II *STANTON HALL*

Drawing room at Stanton Hall.

Carved Carrara marble mantel
located in drawing room at Stanton Hall.

China cabinet containing a set of
old Paris china at Stanton Hall.

Stanton Hall — Photograph showing the height
and beautiful detail of columns.

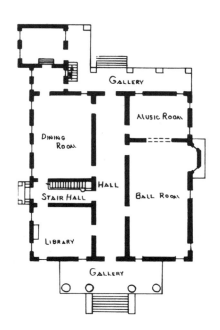

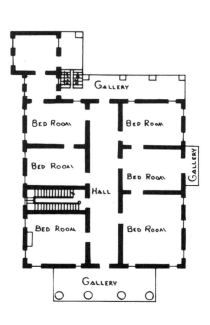

FIRST FLOOR PLAN   SECOND FLOOR PLAN

HAWTHORNE

1814

This house, in which Lafayette was entertained in 1825, is one of the lovely plantation-type houses that were being built throughout the South in 1814.

Its wide gallery across the entire front of the house, its full stairway, its steeply sloping roof and dormer windows must have found their counterpart in many of the better houses of that time—houses that have long since been demolished.

Hawthorne carries out the early Southern type of architecture with unobtrusive beauty. Its outward appearance, for a Southern ante-bellum house, is almost demure.

Its interior, however, is palatial. *Hawthorne* is famous for its pair of double fan doors, with handsome paneling and lights of early blown glass. There are four of these doors—the front and rear entrances to the house, and the doors leading from the hall into the parlor and dining room.

Within, the central hall runs the entire length of the house, the space of which is broken by a stately arch. Behind the arch a stair leads to the upper floor. Among the furnishings in the hall is a French curio cabinet, in which are a cup and saucer, the property of an early Hawthorne owner.

The parlor, which is beautifully furnished, is situated to the left of the hall. The chandelier is of Baccarat crystal. This room has two Belter chairs, and other furniture in rosewood. The rug is a Savonaire with soft shades of yellow, blue and mauve. The drapes are of mauve Italian silk with Brussels lace curtains.

The dining room is on the right of the hall. Furnishings here are of mahogany. Fine silver and glass are among the treasures in this room. Two of the outstanding pieces are a hand-blown glass liquor set and a rosewood cellarette.

From the dining room a door leads to the kitchen, which has an antique French Provincial walnut sideboard. Here, the floor is brick tile.

The master bedroom, also on the first floor, is very roomy, being about 20 feet long. When local upholsterers removed the covering from two sleigh back chairs, an old French bus ticket and a coin dated 1842 were found. These chairs and the rest of the furnishings in this room are of rosewood.

To the rear of the house stands a restored brick kitchen, as well as several other early cottages.

The present owners are Mr. and Mrs. Hyde R. Jenkins who have contributed much to making *Hawthorne* one of the showplaces of Natchez.

Hawthorne is thought to have been built about 1814 by Jonathan Thompson, a young realtor, whose wife was the stepdaughter of Col. Winthrop Sargent, the first territorial governor of Mississippi. Eleven years later, the entire Thompson family was struck down by yellow fever.

Following their deaths, there occurred a series of owners, one of whom was George Overaker, owner of a famous early Natchez tavern. His wife was instrumental in maintaining an orphanage for children of yellow fever victims, and this orphanage has since become the Natchez Protestant Home.

PLATE III *HAWTHORNE*

Parlor at Hawthorne.

Inside doorway and fanlight at Hawthorne.

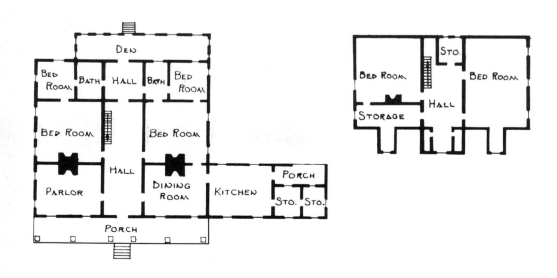

GLOUCESTER

1800

Gloucester, the beautiful Georgian mansion on the Natchez Trace, is famous for having been the home of Winthrop Sargent, first territorial governor of Mississippi. The home was built at the turn of the eighteenth century by the David Williams family, who employed the famous architect, Samuel Young, to supervise its construction. It was purchased in 1808 by Sargent, an upright New Englander, who found it difficult to assimilate the easy customs of Natchez with his Puritanical ideas. Sargent gave *Gloucester* its name from his boyhood home in Massachusetts. Originally it had been called Bellevue, and was the center of 5,000 acres of grounds.

It is a magnificent home in a beautiful mossy setting. Of imposing red brick structure, fronted by a Georgian double gallery, it has four giant white columns. The floor plan of *Gloucester* is unusual. Two identical doors, beautifully lighted, form entrances at either end of the gallery. The doors lead into small hallways, which in turn, lead into a wide corridor which runs parallel to the gallery.

On the inside of the entrance doors are heavy bars. These were essential at the time of *Gloucester's* building, because the home is on the old Natchez Trace, at that time heavily traveled by all kinds of people en route to Natchez.

Both extremities of *Gloucester* are one-half of an octagon, and the interiors of the end rooms reflect this lovely shape. On the west is the large drawing room. Here the mantel is of African black marble carved with columns. Over the mantel is a French gold-leafed mirror. This room has beautiful pieces of period furniture.

On the eastern side, also in the shape of a half-octagon, is the dining room, which has superb china and silver. Among the other rooms on the first floor are a library with many valuable volumes and a music room. *Gloucester* is noted for its fine paintings. Among the masters represented are Salvatore Rosa, Jose Ribera, Francesco Bassi and D'heem.

The house has two handsome curved stairways leading to the second floor, where the bedrooms are located. The most select materials were used in *Gloucester*. Woods are beautifully grained, carvings exquisitely performed. The present owners, the Morrison Family, have done much to enhance the charm of this house.

The former owner was Mrs. Lenox S. Stanton, whose husband was a great-grandson of William Stanton of Windy Hill Manor. William Stanton and his brother, Frederick, were wealthly landowners of early Natchez. Frederick Stanton was the builder of fabulous Stanton Hall.

Gloucester has had its share of laughter, and also its share of sorrow. During the Civil War, a son of Winthrop Sargent, George Washington Sargent, was shot down in the doorway of this house by two Union soldiers. *Gloucester* today, stands proud and haughty, much as it did 170 years ago.

PLATE IV *GLOUCESTER*

Cross Hallway at Gloucester.

One of the entrance doorways at Gloucester.

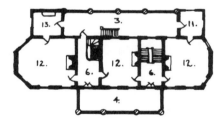

SECOND FLOOR PLAN

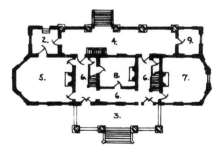

FIRST FLOOR PLAN

1. WINE ROOM
2. SERVING ROOM
3. PORCH
4. GALLERY
5. DINING ROOM
6. HALL
7. DRAWING ROOM
8. LIBRARY
9. TEA ROOM
10. KITCHEN
11. DRESS
12. BED ROOM
13. BATH

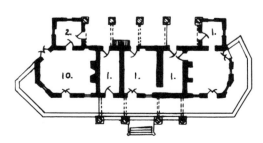

BASEMENT PLAN

TWIN OAKS

1814

This home takes its name from two giant oaks that figured more than a century ago in property deeds in Natchez. One of the original oaks still stands on the front grounds.

Twin Oaks is a lovely unpretentious cottage-type home, with dormer windows and a gallery across the center portion of the house. The pillars are square, and there is a railing around the porch. The house is of brick, painted white. Green blinds against the white of the house beneath tremendous oaks make a peaceful scene.

Twin Oaks was damaged by the Tornado of 1840, which was one of the most severe storms ever to hit Natchez. Many of the fine houses were destroyed or damaged beyond repair, but today there is no evidence of the scars inflicted on *Twin Oaks* by this storm.

Twin Oaks has spacious double parlors opening from a central hall. These parlors are exquisitely furnished in period pieces, many of which were heirlooms in the families of the present owners, Dr. and Mrs. Homer Whittington. Mantels are of plain white marble overhung with Louis XV mirrors. These rooms also have antique French crystal chandeliers. Furniture is of rosewood and mahogany.

The hardware of the doors of *Twin Oaks* is of Sheffield silver. The discovery was made accidentally when a workman, in cleaning the house, spilled acid on a door knob.

At the end of the central hall, and running across the rear of the house, is a large room also used as a parlor. Among other fine pieces in this room is a Steinway grand piano made to special order for a German baroness many years ago.

The dining room in the south wing of the house has magnificent china, silver and glassware. It opens on a small porch, at the foot of which is *Twin Oaks'* famous bulb garden.

Also occupying the first floor is a bedroom and nursery interestingly furnished in pieces of the middle nineteenth century.

The flowers are especially lovely. Mentioned above is the bulb garden which occupies a wide expanse beneath the oaks and is viewed by hundreds every spring. Roses, dahlias, camellias and azaleas are among the flowers nurtured at *Twin Oaks*.

This home has passed through a number of hands throughout the years. The exact date of its building, or the name of its builder, has never been accurately established.

During the Civil War, the Federal troops occupied this house and there is a tale that the soldiers used wispy curtains of fine lace to tether their horses to the trees outside.

Twin Oaks, in its serene setting, offers a sharp contrast to the modern-day hustle and bustle passing at its front door.

PLATE V *TWIN OAKS*

Front parlor at Twin Oaks.

Victorian Slipper Sofa at Twin Oaks.

Louisiana French Desk
at Twin Oaks.

Front bedroom at Twin Oaks.

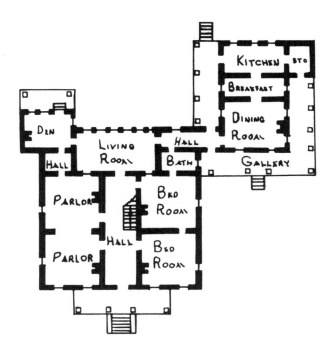

FIRST FLOOR PLAN   SECOND FLOOR PLAN

GREEN LEAVES

Before 1812

Shaded by aged live oak trees, *Green Leaves* spreads over half a city block in a well-populated part of Natchez. In the rear, the grounds go back to Pine Street, hidden from view by a high red brick wall. From the front, on Rankin Street, *Green Leaves* stands on a terraced hill, and is almost obscured by huge azaleas and camellia bushes.

No one knows who built the early part of this house, but records show that it must have been standing in 1812. In 1850 the south wing was added.

The style of architecture is classic. Its entrance has a narrow gallery supported by two large columns. The entrance is effective — a hand carved cypress door with Corinthian pilasters on either side. There are side lights in a circular and rectangular pattern. In the overhead glass, a bullet hole can be seen. Just at the close of the Civil War, bands of marauders stalked Natchez, and one of them took a shot at George Washington Koontz, great-grandfather of the present owner.

Inside is a large entrance hall, to the left of which are double drawing rooms. These rooms have beautifully carved rosewood furniture, black marble mantels, and exquisite gold leaf mirrors. A bedroom is to the right of the hall, and behind the bedroom, a card room.

Two wings extend on either side of the main building. Windows on the front open on wrought-iron balconies. In one wing is the dining room and the most famous of all possessions at *Green Leaves* — its set of china. In blue and gold, each dish is painted with a bird in natural colors.

The paintings on this china are thought to be the work of Audubon, although no pieces are signed. The work is exquisite, and the china takes its place among the finest in Natchez.

The opposite wing contains bedrooms, which are tastefully furnished in the fashion of the day. *Green Leaves* has a two-storied brick kitchen in the rear. The house also has a back gallery reminiscent of colonial style, with windows opening on it from each room. Beyond this is a well-planned courtyard. A swimming pool was built in 1926, making life at *Green Leaves* more pleasant during the summer months.

While it is not known who built the original *Green Leaves*, the site is known to have passed through a number of hands until it was purchased in 1849 by George W. Koontz. Koontz came to Natchez from Pennsylvania, and became affiliated with William Audley Britton in 1836, and in 1861 became a partner in the banking firm of Britton and Koontz.

Koontz was a close friend of Jefferson Davis, president of the Confederacy, and was sent abroad to negotiate loans for the Cause. A daughter married Melchior S. Beltzhoover, who greatly helped the Natchez people in the financial crisis of 1914. Melchior Roch Beltzhoover, grandson of Koontz, married a granddaughter of the Brittons, Miss Ruth Audley Britton Wheeler. This house has been loved and cared for during five generations of the Koontz family.

PLATE VI *GREEN LEAVES*

Dining room at Green Leaves.

Interior doorway at Green Leaves.

Teddy Bear Christmas Tree holding
Teddy Bears that the children of Green Leaves
have had for three generations.

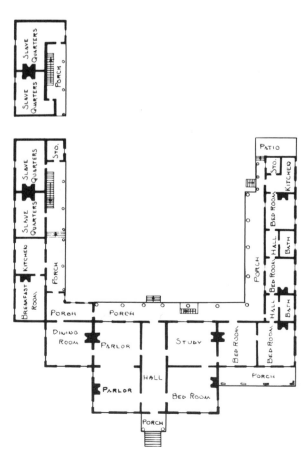

LONGWOOD

1861

If we are to designate a time when Natchez began its years of decline, we must set the date of 1861, the beginning of the Civil War. There was no gradual tapering off — just a shot at Fort Sumter — and an end to the prosperity of Southern planters.

One house in Natchez epitomizes all this — a house that might have ushered in a period of even greater grandeur than the first half of the nineteenth century — *Longwood*, the hollow shell of a Moorish castle that hides itself in primeval forests.

Dr. Haller Nutt, who was building this home for his lovely wife, went to Philadelphia to give his plans to Samuel Sloan, one of the foremost architects of his time.

Nothing in Natchez is even remotely like *Longwood* would have been. Although only the skeleton of the house was ever built, it has endured for over a 100 years, and shows little sign of inward deterioration.

It is six stories high, each story a little smaller than its lower one, until the last floor becomes a tower. There are no halls in the house, which is octagonal in shape. On the ground floor is a rotunda, off which are eight large octagonal rooms — each having an outside entrance. From the main floor to the dome, this rotunda is open and was to have had marble steps encircling it to the cupola.

The lower floor was to house a basement, servants' apartments, game rooms, wine cellar and heating space. The main, or second floor, was planned for a drawing room, banquet hall, library, reception hall, and apartment for the mistress of the house.

Bedrooms would have occupied the third floor, maids' rooms the next floor, a sun parlor the next floor, and finally a glassed-in tower.

Dr. Nutt, a brilliant man, was years ahead of his times. He evolved a series of windows, which would have brought indirect lighting into the rooms. The walls have a system of insulation.

Early work was done by the slaves, but later skilled labor was brought in from Philadelphia. In many of the countries of Europe, orders were placed for statuary, a marble staircase, silver and linens.

Then came the war. When the Philadelphia men heard of it, they dropped their tools, removed their overalls and headed back for the North. Visitors can see the old tools and cans of paint just where they were dropped. How long they will last no one can say. Certainly *Longwood*, or Nutt's Folly as it is sometimes called, has many more years ahead of it.

Dr. Nutt died in 1864, just before the end of the war. Before his death, he had everything boarded up except for the basement floor, and he and his family moved into this. His heirs sold the property in 1968 to Mr. and Mrs. Kelly E. McAdams, who have made many needed repairs so that this interesting house can be viewed by many for years to come.

Just what *Longwood* would have been, many have argued during the past 110 years just as freely as Dr. Nutt's contemporaries must have argued the same question. Certainly *Longwood* is one of the most provocative of all Natchez's past glories — a symbol of what might have been if the planters' world had not changed.

Through the generosity of the McAdams Foundation, *Longwood* was deeded as a gift to the Pilgrimage Garden Club January 29, 1970. In April of 1970, the United States Department of the Interior designated *Longwood* as a National Historical Landmark.

PLATE VII *LONGWOOD*

Balcony at Longwood.

Brick servant quarters at Longwood.

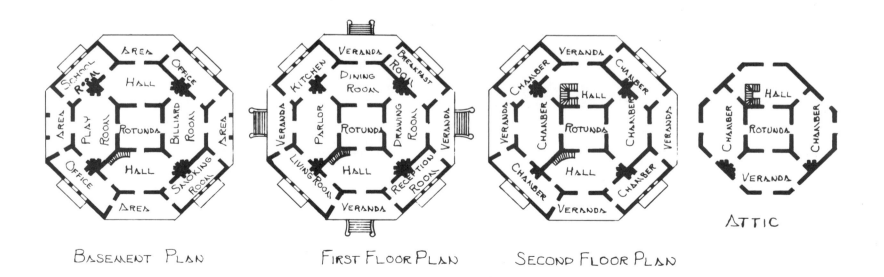

BASEMENT PLAN   FIRST FLOOR PLAN   SECOND FLOOR PLAN

ATTIC

41

ROUTHLAND

Circa 1817

Hidden behind large moss-draped oak trees within a stone's throw of small modern houses, *Routhland* is located on a high hill almost surrounded by deep bayous full of vegetation. On approaching the house, one follows what was once a narrow carriage drive which winds to the summit of a hill. On ascending the summit, the beauty of the well tended grounds forms a most picturesque setting.

Routhland has a long pillared porch with a wide flight of steps rising from a gray and white marble flagged walk. Entering, the main hall extends from front to back. To the left is found the double parlors divided from each other by slender fluted columns. Both rooms have carved white marble mantels and Bristol chandeliers with some of the finest oriental rugs to be found in Natchez. Further enhancing the parlors are two complete sets of Rosewood furniture. A doorway leading from the front parlor takes one to two bedrooms, one of which contains the Walnut bed which was the property of the present owner's grandmother. On the right side of the hall there are two rooms, one being the original library and the other a bedroom. In this room can be found a pink Sienna marble mantel. Behind this room is a small room used as a bedroom. Beyond this wing is a section consisting of two bedrooms. From the large back gallery a doorway opens into a well proportioned dining room. The dining table and the sideboard are of Sheraton design with delicate inlay trim. This room contains many fine pieces of silver and china handed down through the Ratcliff family.

The land surrounding *Routhland* was granted to Job Routh by the Baron Carondelet in 1792. A condition of this land grant required that a dwelling be built upon it within a reasonable length of time or the grantee would forfeit his holdings.

In 1824, *Routhland* was deeded to John Routh, a son of Job. This deed called for ten acres of land and a dwelling. For many years, this house was used as a Summer home by the Routh family.

With the financial crash of 1837, hard times were seen at *Routhland*. In 1842, the house and land were put up for sale by the sheriff of Adams County, Samuel Newman. Dr. Elias Ogden purchased the property at public auction. Within a few days after the sale, Dr. Ogden deeded *Routhland* to Mrs. Routh as a gift giving his love as the consideration. In 1860, *Routhland* was sold by the heirs of Mrs. Routh to Mrs. Eliza Cochran. General Charles Clark purchased *Routhland* in 1871. Clark was a well known figure in Mississippi. He served as Governor from 1864 to 1865 and also as a General in the Confederate Army. After General Clark's death, the property was purchased by his son-in-law, Major William Eugene Montgomery. Again the property changed hands as Major Montgomery gave it to his daughter, Mrs. Emma Winchester. *Routhland* remained in the hands of the Winchesters until the Ratcliff family purchased it in 1944. Much credit is due the Ratcliff family for this meticulous restoration.

PLATE VIII *ROUTHLAND*

Double parlors at Routhland.

Teaster bed with trundle bed
at Routhland.

Main dining room at Routhland.

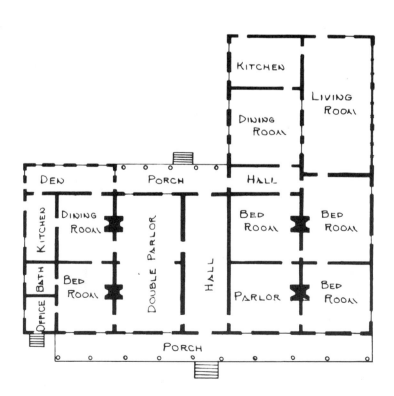

HOPE FARM

1775-1789

Hope Farm, one of the quaintest and most charming of the older houses, is about two-thirds of a mile from downtown Natchez. The house is screened from view from the street by the foliage of ancient shrubs and overlapping branches of trees. Around it is a landscaped garden of azaleas, camellias, myriads of old-fashioned bulbs and large live oak trees.

The sunshiny yellow-colored plaster across the front of *Hope Farm* suggests the theme of this house, which was designed from pleasant entertaining in the days of the Spanish rule of Natchez.

Hope Farm was built in two parts. The earliest one (now the wing, or ell) is shown by records to have been standing in 1775. It was a typical farm house of the times, built of handhewn cypress, and its durability is attested to by the fact that, although it is now 194 years old, its structural timbers are intact and perfectly sound. Wide-railed galleries, front and back, were the order of the day; and with the low-hipped roof, added greatly to the attractiveness of the house.

When the present owners, Mr. and Mrs. J. Balfour Miller, acquired *Hope Farm* in 1926, both sections were in a deplorable condition. Tin tubs were placed throughout to catch rain water that was coming through the roof. Their restoration was handled with great care to preserve all of its original architecture. Its air of gracious and warm hospitality combines with the charm of former days.

The front door opens into the parlor, which is twenty-one feet square, and is connected by large double sliding doors to the dining room, which is twenty-two feet square. On this floor of the front house are the bedrooms occupied by the owners, the den, a large kitchen with an old fireplace and heart cypress cabinets, and the wide back gallery overlooking a brick patio, terraced lawn and garden.

In the den hangs a plaque that was presented to the Millers by the Department of Interior, Washington, D. C., which contains the following:

> "This is to certify that the historical building known as *Hope Farm* has been selected by the Advisory Committee of the Historic American Building Survey as possessing exceptional historical or architectural interest and as being worthy of a most careful preservation for the benefit of future generations and that to this end, a record of its present appearance and condition has been made and deposited for a permanent reference in the Library of Congress."

The two-storied ell is intriguing. Both stories have full length, seventy-foot galleries overlooking terraces with brick steps and masses of colorful flowers which present a sight long to be remembered.

Hope Farm is furnished throughout with priceless antiques representing the period of the times. The rooms have a variety of authentic wall papers and colors, all in keeping with the early Natchez period. Among the outstanding rooms is the Blue Room, admired as an excellent example of the early period in which the house was built.

The name of *Hope Farm* was selected by the Millers from two listed in the deed of 1789 because, when they first acquired the house in 1926, they planned to build it into a small farm. However, they have not carried out their original intention; and for some time they have thought of calling the house by its other early name, Hope Villa.

Mrs. Miller is the originator of the Natchez Pilgrimage, and since its inception in 1932, has devoted most of her time to building it into the now famous annual event.

PLATE IX *HOPE FARM*

Hope Farm — Rear view of the ell
before restoration was begun.
**PHOTO COURTESY OF
MR. AND MRS. J. BALFOUR MILLER**

Dining room and parlor
at Hope Farm.

Bedroom at Hope Farm. Note matching teaster beds.

The Blue Room, an excellent example of the period in which Hope
Farm was built.

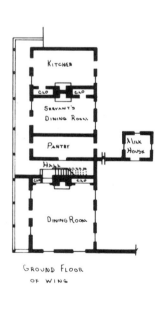

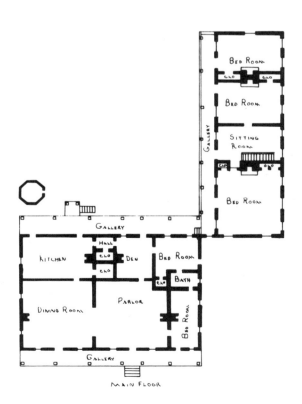

GROUND FLOOR
OF WING

MAIN FLOOR

DUNLEITH

1847

The house that is probably best known to the casual visitor in Natchez is *Dunleith*, which is beautifully visible from one of the main thoroughfares of Mississippi.

Dunleith was built about 1847 on the site of the ruins of one of the most important homes in Natchez — the center of the vast Routh estate. The earlier house was completely destroyed by fire after being struck by lightning, and valuable furnishings collected from Europe were lost.

At the time of the fire, the home was owned by the granddaughter of Job Routh, founder of the Routh fortune — Mrs. Charles Dahlgren, and her husband, said to have been a descendant of King Gustave Adolphus of Sweden.

Dahlgren set out to build a mansion even finer than the one destroyed, and the present *Dunleith* is the result.

Imposing is the word for *Dunleith*, with its double galleries all around the house upheld by grand columns — a fine example of Greek Revival. It was probably influenced by the mansions of the Louisiana sugar planters, for a great similarity can be seen between *Dunleith* and some of the houses of South Louisiana.

The symmetry of *Dunleith* is one of its outstanding points. It is in perfect balance from the tip of its dormer windows, jutting out from a sloping roof, to its finely modeled stairs leading to the lower gallery. Upper and lower entrances are identical.

The interior of the mansion has the typical uniformity of the time — a large central hall, with spacious square rooms on either side. Attached to the building at the rear is a two-storied wing used for a kitchen. Stables and other brick buildings on the grounds date from the first *Dunleith*.

The land around *Dunleith* is spectacular. Occupying forty acres, the grounds slope, first severely and then gently, from the house. Giant oaks and magnolias form a beautiful setting for this mansion, which has been called a Greek temple. Around the estate is a sturdy iron grilled fence placed there by a late owner.

Dunleith passed out of the hands of the Routh family, and eventually became the property of the J. N. Carpenter family. The present owners, Mr. and Mrs. N. L. Carpenter, are the fifth generation of the family to live at *Dunleith*.

PLATE X *DUNLEITH*

Arrangement of columns, south side of Dunleith

Arabesque located in central hall at Dunleith.

Marble mantel located in rear parlor at Dunleith.

Servants quarters as seen from back porch of Dunleith.

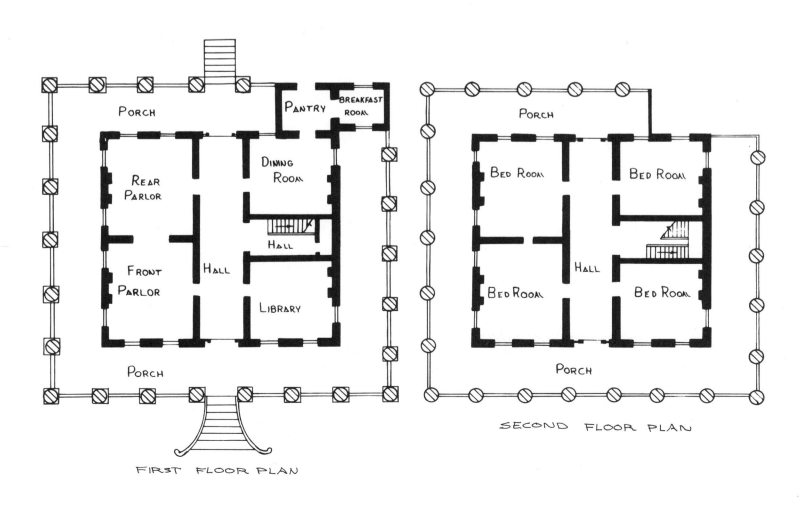

PORCH

PANTRY BREAKFAST ROOM

REAR PARLOR

DINING ROOM

FRONT PARLOR

HALL

HALL

LIBRARY

PORCH

FIRST FLOOR PLAN

PORCH

BED ROOM

BED ROOM

HALL

BED ROOM

BED ROOM

PORCH

SECOND FLOOR PLAN

FAIR OAKS

Circa 1800

From timbers used and the architectural features found in this house, it is believed to be the original house built for Mr. Jesse Carter around 1800. Mr. Carter had come as a child with his family from Virginia to the Natchez region. After attaining manhood, he joined the local militia and soon achieved the rank of Major. He chose for his wife the widow, Sarah Canhard. Mrs. Canhard owned some several hundred acres which had been granted to her first husband by the British Government. After her marriage to Mr. Carter, it was upon this land that their house was constructed. Under the ownership of the Carters, their house had been named Greenoak. Lydia, the daughter of Mr. and Mrs. Carter, married the noted George Poindexter. For a time, Mr. and Mrs. Poindexter lived at Greenoak with the Carters.

George Poindexter was one of the most colorful personalities who ever resided at Greenoak. Mr. Poindexter was one of the rising political figures of the State. His political convictions were deep-seated. When a statement of abuse was overheard by Mr. Poindexter about one of the men he greatly admired, he challenged the maker. At this time a new law had been invoked which made it unlawful to participate in a duel. After alluring several constables, Mr. Poindexter escaped but the challenged man, Mr. Abijah Hunt, was captured and put under arrest. After the release of Mr. Hunt, a note was tended him by Mr. Poindexter establishing a new place and time for the duel. The duel was held across the Mississippi River on the Louisiana Plantation of Stephen Minor and the present day site of the City of Vidalia. Mr. Hunt fell mortally wounded. It has been told that Mr. Poindexter fired before the signal was given. Whether this was a fact or not, Mr. Poindexter fought other duels over this accusa-tion. Mr. Poindexter possessed exceptional legal abilities and it was he who drafted the first Constitution for the State of Mississippi. In 1820, he was elected Governor of the State of Mississippi, being the second man to occupy this office.

In 1836, the property came under the ownership of John Hutchins. It was under his rule that the name of the house was changed to Woodbourn. The property was inherited by the son of Mr. Hutchins and it was sold by him in 1856 to Dr. Orrick Metcalfe. Upon the purchase of the property by Dr. Metcalfe, he changed the name of the house for the third time to *Fair Oaks*. It has been known by this name for one hundred and fourteen years.

Fair Oaks is a Mississippi planter type house, having a porch of unusual length being 98 feet long. The roof is supported by tapered colonettes joined by banisters. The alignment is four colonettes on either side of the wide entrance steps. The doorway is lovely, having a fanlight above and rectangular lights to the sides. Originally the house was only one room deep, having five rooms and a recessed back porch. Through the years when additional living space was needed the back porch was incorporated into the dwelling. One addition of note is the lovely dining room which was added in the 1850's. This room contains a beautiful punkah which hangs above the dining table.

Fair Oaks has remained in the hands of the descendants of Dr. Metcalfe since he purchased the property. This lovely country house was acquired by Mr. and Mrs. Bazile R. Lanneau in 1963. Mr. Lanneau is a great grandson of Dr. Metcalfe. Mr. and Mrs. Lanneau have accomplished an outstanding renovation of this old house which possesses a warmth and charm so typical of a bygone era.

PLATE XI *FAIR OAKS*

Dining room with swinging punkah at Fair Oaks.

Secretary located in parlor at Fair Oaks.

Wig Dresser located in Master bedroom at Fair Oaks.

Bedroom at Fair Oaks.

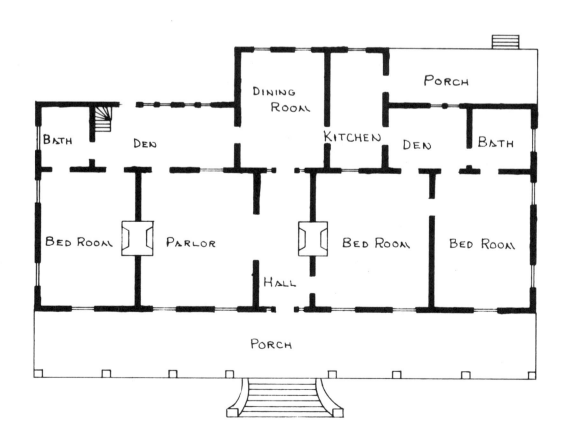

MYRTLE TERRACE

Circa 1830

Myrtle Terrace is one of the charming town houses of Natchez, located in the very shadow of palatial Stanton Hall, sitting on top of a well-terraced hill partially screened from the street by a large magnolia tree and azalea bushes. *Myrtle Terrace* is a raised cottage with a steep sloping roof having three dormers spaced evenly across the front. The roof is supported by six slender columns with railings which enclose a porch that runs the width of the house. The grounds around the house are enclosed by a low brick wall topped with a wrought iron fence of Gothic design. To the rear of the house stands the original brick carriage house and servants' quarters.

Myrtle Terrace was purchased in 1854 by Captain Thomas Leathers, one of the most colorful figures who ever resided in Natchez. Captain Leathers was a giant of a man who made himself a legend in steamboat fame. As master of the steamboat, Natchez, he accepted the challenge of Captain John Cannon, who was master of the

Robert E. Lee, to race from New Orleans, Louisiana, to St. Louis, Missouri. Captain Leathers proclaimed that his steamboat, Natchez, was the fastest on the Mississippi River. On June 30, 1870, the two vessels were made ready for the great race. Bets were placed all over the United States and Europe. Newspaper correspondents were sent to New Orleans to cover the opening of this great race. The steamboats pulled out of New Orleans, the Robert E. Lee was in the lead. Captain Leathers was overconfident and made all of his regular stops. Captain Cannon and his Robert E. Lee surged on up the River and out-distanced the Natchez, arriving at St. Louis some six hours ahead of the Natchez. Captain Leathers arrived behind his challenger but he had not endangered the lives of his passengers or the loss of his cargo.

Today *Myrtle Terrace* is owned by Mr. McVey Butler and is enjoyed by all members of the Butler family. The house is in the same prime condition that it was when the master of the house was the remarkable Captain Leathers.

PLATE XII *MYRTLE TERRACE*

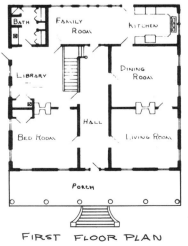

FIRST FLOOR PLAN

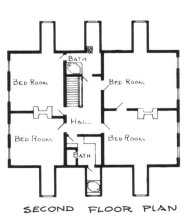

SECOND FLOOR PLAN

MELROSE

1845-1847

The earlier houses of Natchez, though sturdily built, were planned for comfort without too much thought for embellishment. But in 1845, when Mississippi's well-known lawyer, John T. McMurran, built *Melrose*, attention was being given to the minutest detail.

Melrose has been called the "most professional" of all the houses in Natchez. It is built of red brick, with a massive white double gallery — a blend of Georgian and Greek Revival.

The McMurrans spared no expense in erecting *Melrose*. Bricks were burned on the place, and sand used in the construction was brought from central Mississippi. There is a large hall, from which open double drawing rooms, and behind that a library — all connected with double doors so that they can be converted into one massive wing.

The lighting of the hall is impressive. Small candles, now electrified, are placed over the doorways. The front drawing room is noted for its Egyptian black marble mantel. Over the mantel is a magnificent French mirror which has been there since the house was furnished.

The Civil War was a hard blow to the McMurrans, as it was to many others in Natchez. In 1865 Melrose was acquired by George Malin Davis, another outstanding lawyer. *Melrose* has been in the hands of descendants of the Davis family since that time, and still has many of the original furnishings, plus fine additions.

The present owner is Mrs. George M. D. Kelly, widow of the grandson of the original Davis. Mr. Kelly inherited *Melrose* at the age of eight, but it was not until after his marriage that he and Mrs. Kelly came to Natchez to inspect the house in 1901.

Although it had been closed for twenty years, Mrs. Kelly was so impressed by the beauty of the architecture and furnishings that the couple moved to Natchez and began to restore *Melrose* to its original splendor. The exterior of the house is still as it was when constructed.

Melrose has many treasures, among them an original Audubon of Natchez that had gone begging for years before it was finally procured by the Davises. It is impossible to describe all the beautiful pieces in *Melrose*. Visitors are always impressed with a marble inlay table in bird design. The eyes of the birds were once jeweled, but the original stones have been missing for many years.

Another item of particular interest is the solid mahogany punkah in the dining room — the most famous in Natchez.

The grounds of *Melrose* are breath-taking. There is a pond with some of the few cypress trees to be found in hilly Natchez, a large variety of shrubbery and acres of well-clipped grass.

PLATE XIII *MELROSE*

Front parlor with unusual swiveled game chair at Melrose.

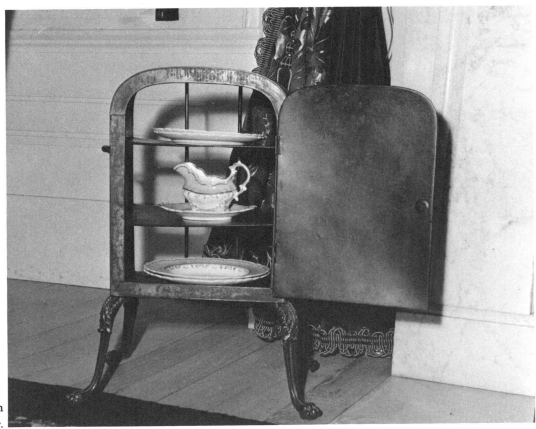

Food warmer located in
dining room at Melrose.

Melrose — Rear view with kitchen and servant quarters.

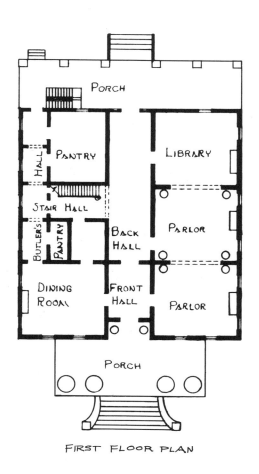

FIRST FLOOR PLAN

SECOND FLOOR PLAN

CHEROKEE

1799-1810

In the days of the Spanish rule in Natchez, yellow-fever was a grim scourge — striking down entire families within the space of a few days, sparing neither the rich nor the poor, the people of Natchez-Under-the-Hill, or of Natchez above.

As the people searched for the cause of the fever, many ideas that now seem ridiculous became laws. One of these laws was that no excavation could be done, for it was feared that removal of dirt spread the disease.

Because of that law, one of the most admired houses in Natchez came into being — *Cherokee.* The law against excavation has long been repealed, and the land surrounding *Cherokee's* grounds were brought to city level. However, to prevent excavation at that time, *Cherokee* was built into the side of the hill; and this blend of architecture into terrain is what gives *Cherokee* one of the most delightful floor plans of any house in Natchez. *Cherokee* now sits atop a hill, with the street below.

The original part of the house was built in 1794 by Jessie Greenfield, member of a prominent early Natchez family. This section is now the rear of the house.

It was made of brick — two stories, unusually long, and only one room deep. The three rooms on the lower floor were built flush with the ground and paved with brick in the manner of the Spanish builders.

In 1810 the house had passed into the hands of David Michie, famed restaurateur of that period. Michie built around the Spanish portion of the house a complete new front of Greek Revival, and although the house is of two periods and two entirely different types of architecture, the blend is perfect.

The accompanying photograph will show that *Cherokee* has a recessed gallery, a "different" idea in Natchez houses. It has the austere Grecian columns, and a lovely front doorway.

Inside is a foyer, with a wide parlor to the left, and a large dining room to the right. Directly behind the foyer is the most interesting room in the house, a large music room, which is part of the original house.

Little hallways off the music room go in opposite directions, into bedrooms. In one hall is *Cherokee's* beautiful and famous mahogany spiral stairway.

Going downstairs from the music room is what was probably a kitchen in former days, and this leads to a brick patio.

Cherokee has beautiful furnishings, ranking with the finest in Natchez. Purchased in a state of disrepair, *Cherokee* has been authentically and beautifully restored by the present owners, Mr. and Mrs. Charles J. Byrne.

PLATE XIV *CHEROKEE*

Front parlor at Cherokee.

Bedroom at Cherokee.

Inside doorway separating entrance hall from rear parlor at Cherokee.

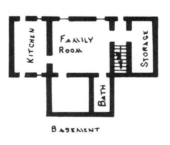

BASEMENT

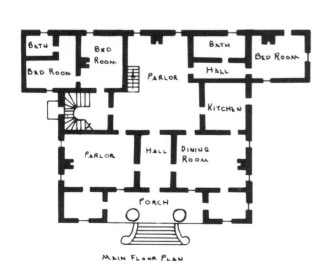

MAIN FLOOR PLAN

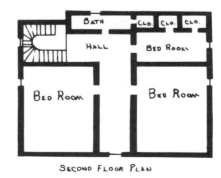

SECOND FLOOR PLAN

HOLLY HEDGES

1796

A person seeking a glimpse backward into the life of a Natchez family when the Spanish were in power would do well to visit *Holly Hedges*.

This house, not far from the business district of Natchez, is a raised cottage — that is, a one and one-half story building with a basement. It is of cypress, built in 1796.

The house was remodeled in 1832 when Judge Edward Turner, a prominent Natchez man of those days, bought it. Though it passed through the hands of several families, it was not until 1948, when it was purchased by the Earl Hart Millers, that restoration began.

The Millers are outstanding decorators, and every item that has been used in the restoration is a fine piece of its period.

Holly Hedges was built by Don Juan Scott, and the original deed, in archaic Spanish, has been kept. Scott, who with his brother was instrumental in bringing a number of settlers to this part of the country from the East, was granted the land by the Spanish crown on the condition that he be remarried in the Catholic church (he was evidently a Protestant), that he promise not to leave Natchez, and that he have no bull fights in his side yard.

Its exterior is simple. It sits close to the street, has a central door with two windows on either side, dormer windows above and side chimneys creating perfect balance.

As one enters the foyer at *Holly Hedges*, the three matching fanlighted doors through the center portion of the house immediately catch the eye. The rear of this hall is used as the formal dining room. The walls of this room have been covered with mural wallpaper depicting Early American scenes.

The floor plan of the house itself follows the pattern of many of the earlier homes. It has a parlor, a lovely wood-paneled library, smaller dining room and kitchen on one side of the house, and on the other three bedrooms. Extending between the kitchen and back bedroom is an airy gallery opening onto a brick paved patio.

Original gutters on the house were of hollowed-out cypress saplings. Through the years, as the gutters decayed and the roof began to leak, water poured into the basement. The mud of generations began to accumulate and to harden.

One day Mrs. Miller thought she saw the outlines of a pattern about nine inches square on the dirt floor of the basement. She began to excavate and turned up an original Spanish tile, unglazed, handmade in Natchez, gray in color — 173 years old. The entire basement floor proved to be of this tile.

Thus the Millers began restoration of the basement, which is now one of the most interesting parts of the house. The basement has in it an old cistern, which was locked. Previous residents feared pollution of the water. The cistern was dug out and drained, and found to be 35 feet deep. An electric light was installed in the bottom and a circular brick wall built around the top.

The basement also has the original Indian guards, that is, the wooden bars inserted in the casements of the windows.

When purchased, *Holly Hedges* was in a deplorable state of disrepair, but the Millers have recreated the hospitable simplicity of early Natchez days.

PLATE XV *HOLLY HEDGES*

Corner cabinet in dining room
at Holly Hedges.

Fireplace in basement
at Holly Hedges.

Fanlight above the rear doorway of entrance hall at Holly Hedges.

GARCONNIERE

BRICK COURTYARD

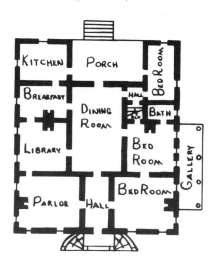

ELMSCOURT

1810

Amid a group of colonial and classic homes, *Elmscourt* is the "Different" one — the home that was changed to take on an air of the Mediterranean countries.

Built about 1810 by an English couple, and acquired a few years later by the first sheriff of Adams County, Louis Evans, this house was a square, solidly constructed, two-story planters'-type house with wide double galleries.

In 1830 it was acquired by Mr. and Mrs. Ayers P. Merrill as a wedding gift from Mrs. Merrill's father, Frank Surget, one of the few really wealthy men in the United States at that time. Merrill was a friend of Ulysses S. Grant, and at one time was the United States Minister to Belgium.

Using the square house as a center base, the Merrills added two one-story wings on either side. They tore out the colonial structure on the galleries, and imported from Italy the grillwork which is shown in the accompanying photograph. This grillwork is classed with the most beautiful in Natchez. It has a grape design which is carried out in arches and fretwork. Across the front and sides of each porch are wrought iron banisters.

The interior of *Elmscourt* has a hall through the center, with double parlors to the left. In this wing are also a smoking room and billiard hall. A music room, banquet hall and library are on the right. The upstairs consists entirely of bedrooms.

Elmscourt is now owned by Mrs. Douglas H. MacNeil, daughter of the late Mr. and Mrs. David McKittrick. Mrs. McKittrick was a Surget, a family of very prominent land-owners in the Natchez country.

Although the original furnishings are no longer at *Elmscourt*, the McKittrick family and their heirs have added many pieces from their own families' homes of long ago. A period piece of especial note is a serving table bearing the coat-of-arms of the Duke of Devonshire in England. It is carved in a black snake design.

Elmscourt also has a handmade punkah. Among the other fine details are white marble mantels carved in grape design to match the carving on the outside grillwork, beautiful vases, pottery, mirrors and fine bronze chandeliers.

The chandeliers, which hold hundreds of tiny candles, were the inspiration for "The Ball of a Thousand Candles," an annual ball given in the early days of the Natchez Pilgrimage. This event has now been discontinued.

To the rear of *Elmscourt* stands an interesting stable and carriage house as well as other buildings of note.

Amidst its vast acreage *Elmscourt* stands, white and magnificent, against a background of towering moss-hung oaks.

PLATE XXVI   *ELMSCOURT*

Double parlor at Elmscourt.

Entrance doorway at Elmscourt.

Dining room with punkah at Elmscourt.

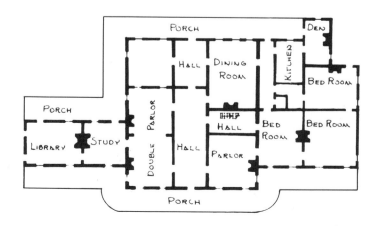

ELGIN PLANTATION

1780-1840

Elgin is another of the Natchez homes that was begun in Spanish times and added to in later years, so that the early part of the house loses its identity as Spanish, and becomes a typical Natchez plantation home.

The earliest part of *Elgin* was built before 1780, and it has low ceilings of the Spanish period. It was in 1840, however, that the front of *Elgin* was added around the older part by Dr. John Carmichael Jenkins, a famous horticulturist.

Elgin is a true frame plantation house. It has large double galleries, ninety feet in width, supported by eight columns, across the entire house. The roof slopes sharply to the columns. Railings across the front galleries and wide stairs give the house a gentle, hospitable look.

Elgin also has the Jib doors beneath all windows opening on the upper and lower galleries to let in the breezes. These doors are hinged on both sides, and open in the center, to allow a maximum of ventilation.

Elgin's double parlors have high ceilings, showing that it was built when Natchez residents had learned that the humid weather of the South became stifling under the low Spanish-type ceilings. On the wall between the parlors is a huge black marble fireplace, and on either side of the fireplace are tremendous double folding doors that reach from the floor to the ceiling. The furnishings here are authentic, many of them having been in the family of the present owner, Mrs. James W. Lambert. Mrs. Lambert has among many other fine pieces, two of unusual note — one an old type kerosene lamp, and the other a Grand-father's clock made about 1720 by Hadwin of Liverpool, England.

Opposite the parlors and to the right of the usual hall which is found in many of the floor plans in Natchez, is the library, also high-ceilinged, and also boasting a black marble mantel.

It is in the dining room, which lies at the end of the hall, that one sees the truly old part of the house. This is the part built about 1780, and it has the low Spanish ceiling. The dining room also has an oaken punkah, hand-hewn and suspended above the table.

The unusually large bedrooms are reached by an interesting mahogany stairway, which Jefferson Davis once trod to sleep in one of the beds.

A sketch of *Elgin* is incomplete without a few words about its fruit orchards, which in the middle of the nineteenth century were famous throughout this area. Dr. Jenkins was interested in grafting trees; and he kept a record of his graftings, which reveals many interesting experiments — among them a cross between a quince and a pear. Years ahead of the times, Dr. Jenkins experimented with transporting fruits in ice from Natchez to the North by boat.

The older Jenkinses were victims of yellow fever in 1855, but *Elgin* was in the hands of descendants of the Jenkins family until 1914.

Because of the fineness and solidity of the wood and the workmanship, *Elgin* is one of the frame houses that has endured through the years.

PLATE XVII   *ELGIN PLANTATION*

Elgin Plantation as it appeared in 1880.   COURTESY MR. AND MRS. F. N. GEDDES

English silver tea set at Elgin Plantation.

Elgin Plantation jib door.
Note how the lower section of the window opens into small doors.

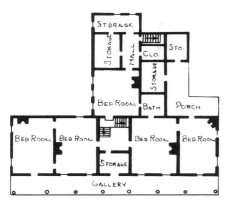

SECOND FLOOR PLAN

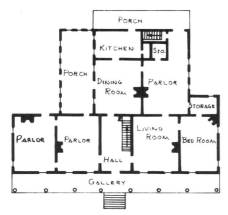

FIRST FLOOR PLAN

MOUNT REPOSE

1824

On far-fetched events of years ago, today's life hinges. For example, because Henry Clay was not elected President of the United States, the grounds of *Mount Repose* are entered from the side. The story goes that the builder of *Mount Repose*, in planning the grounds, said he would make a drive straight to the door only if his friend Clay were elected President . . . . but Clay was not.

This is only one of the many stories of famous people that this lovely home could tell. It was built by William Bisland in 1824 on land from an original Spanish grant, which he inherited from his grandfather, a famous cotton planter.

At the time that *Mount Repose* was built, the Georgian influence was seeping into Natchez. But *Mount Repose* is not Georgian. It is simply a beautiful early plantation home, two stories high, with expansive porches.

Situated on a small hill facing moss-hung oaks, it has an almost unbelievable Southern setting. The double porches are large and airy, the entrance beautifully set with fan-shaped overhead lights and rectangular side lighting. On either side of the central portion are one-storied wings.

Mount Repose was built to take advantage of Southern air and to withstand the hot summer weather. The hall inside is two stories high, inviting the cool breezes through the building. In the rear is an enclosed stairway to the second floor.

Descendants of the Bisland family have always occupied *Mount Repose*. The present owners are Mr. and Mrs. J. Ferd Sessions. Under their direction, a varied assortment of shrubs and trees native to this region have been planted. Mrs. Sessions has a deep feeling for this house as it was here that she was born and reared.

Because the home has never gone out of the family, it now contains many interesting historical records, as well as numerous fine authentic pieces. One heirloom is a cherry desk made by a slave cabinet-maker. This desk was once the property of Judge W. B. Shields, who was a famous figure in Aaron Burr's trial for treason.

A descendant of the early Bisland, Miss Elizabeth Bisland, became a famous newspaper woman. Her biography of Lafcadio Hearn is well known, but old-timers will best remember her for her race around the world with Nellie Bly.

Mount Repose is no longer on one of the great United States highways, but when it was built, it stood by the side of what was then the famous King's Highway, which followed the Mississippi River on its eastern bank.

PLATE XVIII *MOUNT REPOSE*

Portion of parlor at Mount Repose.

Bedroom at Mount Repose. Note wood grain in floors.

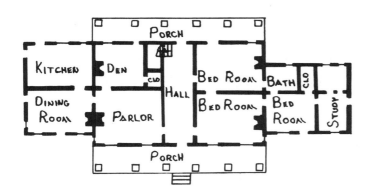

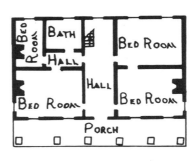

EDGEWOOD

Circa 1850

Edgewood is another of the fine houses that was built for a member of the Bisland Family. Located in the vicinity of the Pine Ridge settlement, a short distance out of Natchez, constructed on part of one of the original land grants received by John Bisland from the Spanish Government in 1782. Adjoining Mount Repose Plantation to the West, the property was given to Mr. and Mrs. Samuel Hopkins Lambdin by the father of Mrs. Lambdin, who was the Master of Mount Repose. In choosing a suitable location for their house, they chose the summit of a hill with a vista in all directions.

In designing *Edgewood*, Mrs. Lambdin wanted something different. The design of her home must not follow the established pattern which was being used so abundantly in this region at that time.

Edgewood is basically of Georgian design which has been embellished with steamboat Gothic ornamentation. Built of plantation-made brick which were burned on the place, the exterior walls are stuccoed with a soft shade of salmon pink. The woodwork shows that there must have been fine craftsmen retained to do the finish. When the Lambdins had *Edgewood* constructed, their prime interest must have been to build a house that would be comfortable and that would endure the ravages of time.

In viewing the facade of *Edgewood*, it appears that it is a two-storied house. From the rear, it shows that it has three floors. Originally the first floor was used for storage, servants' quarters and a kitchen. All of this area has been remodeled and is used as living quarters and a recreation space.

Edgewood is one of the few houses built in this period that contained a running water system within its interior. Water was pumped into tanks located in the attic from the two large cisterns to the rear of the house. This water supply was piped to several locations within the house.

Another item of interest is the original dumb waiter which permitted hot food from the kitchen to be elevated to the serving room adjacent to the dining room which is on the second floor.

In 1951, Mr. and Mrs. Richard A. Campbell purchased *Edgewood*. With this property transfer, a century of rule by the Lambdin Family of this estate was brought to a close. Under the ownership of Mr. and Mrs. Campbell, *Edgewood* has been returned to, if not surpassing, its former grandeur. Within the rooms of this house are some of the rarest eighteenth century English antiques to be found in this region. Various pieces of this furniture can be classified as museum pieces. Even though the Campbells have transformed this house into an elegant showplace, it is used as a home and is enjoyed by all who visit here.

PLATE XIX *EDGEWOOD*

Parlor at Edgewood.

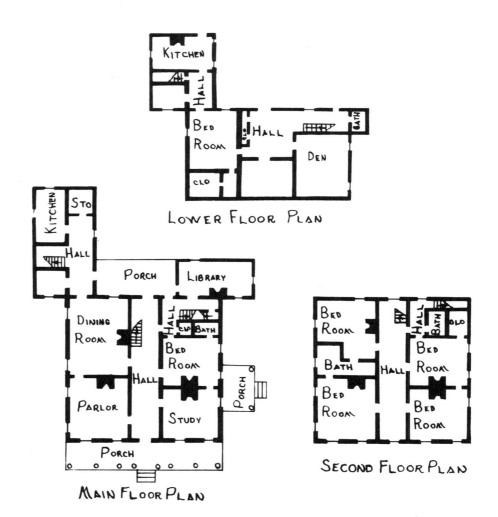

KITCHEN

HALL

BED ROOM

HALL

BATH

DEN

CLO

LOWER FLOOR PLAN

KITCHEN STO

HALL

PORCH LIBRARY

DINING ROOM

HALL BATH CLO

BED ROOM

HALL PORCH

PARLOR

STUDY

PORCH

MAIN FLOOR PLAN

BED ROOM

HALL BATH CLO

BATH

BED ROOM

HALL

BED ROOM

BED ROOM

SECOND FLOOR PLAN

Dining room at Edgewood.

MISTLETOE

1807

Mistletoe is one of the quaintest small houses to be found in the Natchez region, located on what was once called the Selsertown Road in the Pine Ridge section.

This house can claim no stated architectural pattern. It can best be described as a Mississippi planter's house. Rooms are irregular in size, and fireplaces are located in a corner of each of the two front rooms. The failure to follow any established form of architecture has enhanced the charm of this early house.

John and Susannah Bisland had *Mistletoe* constructed for their oldest son, Peter, upon his marriage to Barbara Foster in 1807. John Bisland cut away some of the land granted him by the Spanish crown in 1788 and also gave this to him.

After 21 years of a peaceful life spent at *Mistletoe*, Peter was found dead. His body was located by servants in one of the cisterns (a large brick and cement underground reservoir which contained rain water). Peter had been ill, and being weakened, must have fallen to his death trying to draw water from the cistern. *Mistletoe* was sold to Dr. Mathew Atchison in 1842. Within a few years the house was reacquired by members of the Bisland family. The present owner, Mr. S. H. Lambdin III, is the great-great-grandson of John Bisland. The late Mrs. Lambdin was an authority on flowers of the South and spent many hours of her life developing the grounds around *Mistletoe* into one of the most beautiful spots in the county. Because of her profound knowledge of horti-culture, the gardens are filled with many rare plants which give a profusion of color and delightful fragrance in spring and summer. Under the watchful eye of Mr. Lambdin, the gardens continue to receive expert care.

A broad walk laid with slave-made brick, bordered by dwarf youpons, leads to a balustraded porch extending across the front of the house. The roof is supported by four square wooden pillars. Opening into the main hall is a double colonial door with a carved fan-light flanked by side lights of rectangular glass panes. To the rear of this hall is another classic double doorway with a lovely fan-light. On the right of the hall is a bedroom furnished with early period pieces. To the left of the hall is the parlor sheathed with horizontal cypress boards. In this room, too, are fine pieces of furniture as well as family portraits. Furnishings of Chippendale, Queen Anne, and Hepplewhite design are heirlooms of the Lambdin and Henderson families.

Two wings were added in 1947. These wings were built to look like the two small outer buildings which originally faced each other across the lower patio. One building was the kitchen; the other, slave quarters. With this addition the wings form a "U" shape to the rear of the house. This space has been effectively developed into a most attractive patio.

Mistletoe is deceptive in size; as it is much more spa-cious than one would believe. This charming house has been effectively restored. Mrs. Lambdin's knowledge and love of antiques had enabled her to utilize many objects of beauty. The Lambdins have created a warmth of atmos-phere here than many attempt but comparatively few accomplish.

PLATE XX *MISTLETOE*

ARLINGTON

1816

Arlington is one of the perfect examples of Georgian architecture in the South; yet it is Georgian adapted to Southern climates, with the ceilings raised very high.

This massive house, situated on seventy-five acres of land in the heart of Natchez, possesses detail work among the finest in the city.

Arlington is a red-brick structure, fronted by a double gallery upheld by four stately Doric columns. In many of the Natchez houses, the brick was made on the grounds by slaves; but the brick for *Arlington* was imported from England.

All four main doorways to *Arlington* are of note. Above are tremendous fan lights, and both these and the side lights are in magnificent design.

The front steps, and all window and door facings and mantels in the house are of marble. The house is really four stories high, having a basement and an attic. Downstairs is a large hall with two rooms on either side. The hall rises seventeen and one-half feet in height.

The house was built by a widow, Mrs. Jane Surget White. Stories have been told that Mrs. White's death was mysterious, and that she died the day following a grand ball given in honor or the opening of the home.

However, Mrs. Anne Vaughn, the present owner of *Arlington,* states that this story is without foundation; and that the real romance of *Arlington* lies in the normal lives of the successive families who lived there in the 153 years of its existence — in their births, growing up, marriages, and deaths.

The late Mrs. Hubert Barnum, mother of the present owner, was the first president of the Pilgrimage Club. It was through her efforts that has made *Arlington* into a show-place that is almost a museum. She had a collection of nearly 1,000 dolls, as well as an antique doll house. Among collections of china, books, silver, and lovely period furniture, her collection of glass is fabulous.

On its grounds are some of the oldest and finest shrubbery in Natchez. There is one row of pale pink azaleas that a former owner brought from China many years ago. Since then, that variety has been propagated throughout Natchez and this entire section. Among the camellia bushes on the estate is one that is thought to be the tallest of its kind in the country. This camellia "tree" rises half way up the lower sash of the second story window.

Arlington now sits on its acreage like an island within the heart of Natchez, a step from Main Street.

PLATE XXI *ARLINGTON*

Castiron lamp-post at Arlington,
cast at Natchez in the 1840s.

Entrance doorway at Arlington.

Interior doorway at Arlington.

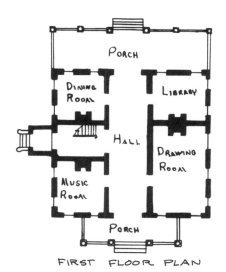

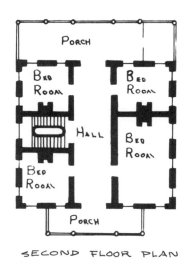

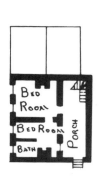

FIRST FLOOR PLAN

SECOND FLOOR PLAN

93

THE SMITH HOUSE

Circa 1840

In 1795, James Cole petitioned the Spanish Government for a grant to the lot where this brick story and a half house stands. In his petition he stated that he was a carpenter and that he desired to build a house in the New City of Natchez. In 1807, Cole's claim to this lot was rejected as an unrecorded Spanish grant was presented in the name of James Ross. This lot had been conveyed to Samuel P. Moore in 1799 by Ross. However, by some means, the Coles retained title to this property as it was sold by members of that family in 1833. The building firm of Neibert and Gimmell acquired the property and operated a lumber yard on part of the lot. While Neibert and Gimmell owned the property, it is believed that they constructed the present house. A judgement was levied on the firm and this property was put up for public sale by the sheriff of Adams County in 1842. Samuel Burns tended the highest bid and took over as the new owner. The house was occupied by the Burns family until they sold it in 1872 to Mrs. Marx (Sarah) Lemle. Andrew J. Smith befriended Mrs. Lemle and upon her death she willed the property to him. Today the house is owned and occupied by Mr. and Mrs. John F. Smith. The appearance of this house is always superb with its well clipped hedge and its warm yellow color partially shaded by oak and dogwood trees. This is one of the fine examples of a Natchez town house of the 1840's.

PLATE XXII *THE SMITH HOUSE*

DIXIE

1795-1821

Dixie is the house that no one would have due to its deplorable condition. The interior floors had rotted away and brick walls had cracked and begun to crumble. Much of the fine woodwork had been exposed to the elements for years. What the exposure to the elements didn't destroy, vandals did. Basically all that was left was a shell.

With foresight and the ability to visualize what could be done, Mr. and Mrs. Tom L. Ketchings purchased the property in 1963. With a battery of skilled workmen, gradually the restoration got underway. For two full years the Ketchings, with meticulous attention to detail, oversaw the work. Fine millwork was ordered that was an exact copy of the original patterns. Nearly all window and door casings had to be replaced as well as new window sashes. Masons restored the delapidated brick walls and plasterers came in to begin the job of lathing and plastering the interior. Thus the Ketchings completed a fine restoration that so many felt could never be accomplished.

It is thought that the oldest part of *Dixie* was constructed in 1795. This section was part of a dependency to an earlier house. This plot of ground was granted to Maurice Stockpoole by the Spanish Government in 1794. In order for a person to retain his grant in these times, he had to build a dwelling on the land and inhabit it within one year. Therefore, Mr. Stockpoole must have

built a house on this lot in 1795.

Mr. Samuel Davis had the present *Dixie* built in 1821 incorporating part of the early house in this new home. Members of the Davis Family resided here until the property was sold in 1852 by Mr. Davis. After this sale the property changed hands many times through the years.

The central hall, which runs from front to back, is divisioned off midway by huge sliding doors. On the left of the hall is the parlor and behind this is the dining room and kitchen. To the rear of the kitchen is a den which extends into a wing. On the right of the hall are two lovely bedrooms. In the one to the rear is a massive bed said to have belonged to the famous steamboat Captain, T. P. Leathers. Throughout the house are fine furnishings, some of which have been handed down for generations in both Mr. and Mrs. Ketchings' families.

To the back of the hall on the right is a stair leading to the second floor which consists of two bedrooms and baths and a small sitting room.

Dixie is located in one of the oldest sections of Natchez. For its neighbors it has the Governor Holmes House, Griffith-McComas house, Holly Hedges and Texada Tavern.

The restoration of *Dixie* and its gardens have kept this historic house from slipping into oblivion.

PLATE XXIII *DIXIE*

Master bedroom at Dixie.

Rear view of Dixie showing pattern of original garden.

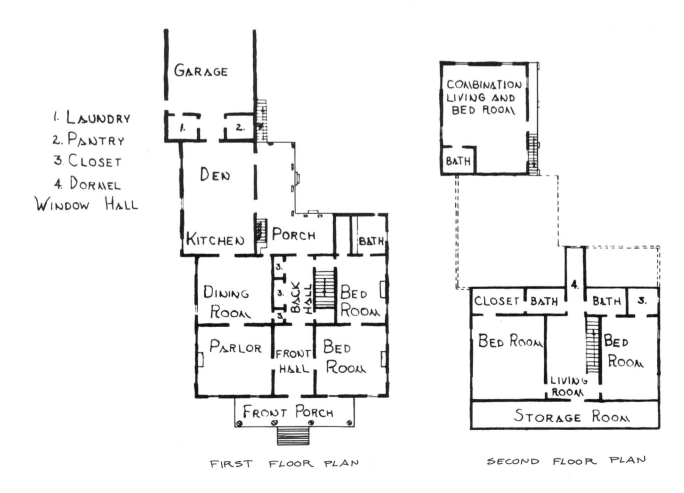

1. LAUNDRY
2. PANTRY
3. CLOSET
4. DORMEL
WINDOW HALL

GARAGE

1.   2.

DEN

KITCHEN   PORCH   BATH

3.

DINING   3.   BED
ROOM   BACK   ROOM
        HALL
        3.

PARLOR   FRONT   BED
        HALL   ROOM

FRONT PORCH

FIRST FLOOR PLAN

COMBINATION
LIVING AND
BED ROOM

BATH

CLOSET BATH   4.   BATH   3.

BED ROOM   BED
        ROOM

        LIVING
        ROOM

STORAGE ROOM

SECOND FLOOR PLAN

CONNELLY'S TAVERN

1795

History was made at *Connelly's Tavern* when the first United States flag was raised on its hill in 1797 in the very shadow of the flag of Spain floating on the nearby hill of Fort Rosalie.

It is a stirring thing to see this house which has been faithfully restored to its place in American history. *Connelly's Tavern* was first built as a residence about 1795, while the Spanish held Natchez. At its foot runs the Old Natchez Trace, the important roadway that linked the eastern United States with the West.

It is an excellent example of Spanish Provincial architecture. Built partly of brick and partly of wood, it is believed to have been constructed of timbers from boats that were floated down the river, carrying merchandise, and sold at Natchez. The timbers are still solid, and the ancient workmanship so fine that after more than a century and a half, the building is as sturdy as rock.

Connelly's Tavern first began to figure in American history when Andrew Ellicott arrived from Washington, D. C., to place on the map Parallel 31 for the United States. Although a treaty had been signed with Spain, the Spaniards refused to evacuate their garrison at Fort Rosalie.

Ellicott, having made *Connelly's Tavern* his headquarters, raised the flag of the United States on this hill. A year later Isaac Guion, of American Revolution fame, arrived in Natchez and also made this hill his headquarters. It was Guion who, through a coup, made the Spaniards evacuate, and claimed this territory for the United States of America.

It was at *Connelly's Tavern*, a decade later, that Aaron Burr is said to have come when making his plans in this section of the country. Certainly throughout the years many famous personages have stopped at the Tavern.

Through the years, *Connelly's Tavern* passed through the hands of many owners and finally, after the Civil War, like many of the other houses, began to fall into hard times. It was strong, but bedraggled, when the Natchez Garden Club purchased it in 1935 and began its restoration.

The restoration was slow, because members wanted only authentic furnishings — preferably from Natchez. Richard Koch, famous architectural consultant from New Orleans, was engaged.

Today *Connelly's Tavern* is a unique house, having galleries along the upper and lower floors supported by nine colonnettes to each gallery and flanked by wooden railings.

Downstairs are the kitchen and tap room, among others, and upstairs the bedrooms, dining room and ballroom. The furnishings are museum pieces — each with its own history. One is the church bench on which Aaron Burr sat, when he was being arraigned for treason against the United States, under the oak trees at Washington, Mississippi. In the tap room is a hand-carved cypress bar from a tavern of Natchez-Under-the-Hill.

Architects from all sections of the country have been entranced with the thought that such a house could have been built in the wilderness at a time when even the wealthy were living in square houses of raw timber.

PLATE XXIV *CONNELLY'S TAVERN*

Connelly's Tavern as it appeared in 1935.

Tap Room at Connelly's Tavern. The bench that Aaron Burr sat on during his arraignment for treason against The United States is in this room.

Parlor at Connelly's Tavern.

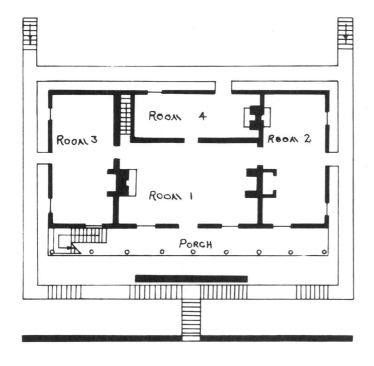

FIRST FLOOR PLAN

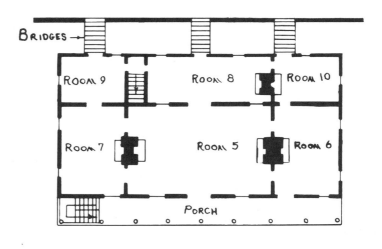

SECOND FLOOR PLAN

MONMOUTH

1818

Monmouth, once the home of Governor John A. Quitman of Mississippi, is a stately house, solid in detail, sturdy in structure.

In common with many Southern homes of this period, its facade has a two-storied gallery supported by four gigantic columns. One difference is noted — the columns are square instead of round. The gallery on the upper floor has picturesque banisters.

Monmouth is a massive house with massive rooms. It is built of brick on the top of a sloping hillock. It was erected about 1818 by a Mr. and Mrs. John Hankinson, an unfortunate couple who died shortly after moving into their house. Their death resulted from yellow fever, which they contracted from a sick traveler whom they befriended.

The house was sold and eventually, in 1826, was purchased by John A. Quitman.

The Quitmans furnished the house in grandiose style. He had a fine collection of books, and she had exquisite china. The house was also well known for its paintings, an outstanding one having been of Mrs. Quitman leading the grand march in Natchez with Lafayette before she was married.

The doors of *Monmouth* are especially lovely, with beautiful overhead and side lights. A much admired feature is the Adam style carved woodwork.

Quitman was one of the most famous statesman this section has produced. He was a major general in the Mexican War, leading a group of Mississippians to battle, and eventually raising the United States flag over the Mexican capital.

His popularity was so great that upon his return to Mississippi, he was elected governor of the state. Although he later resigned during a furor because of his Cuban sympathy, he was elected to the United States Congress, and was presented a sword by Congress for his gallantry in Mexico.

But tragedy struck down Quitman while he was at the height of his career. Some say he was poisoned at a banquet given for President Buchanan in 1859. At any rate, he returned to *Monmouth*, where he died a lingering death.

Subsequently other owners occupied *Monmouth*, and it finally came to the hands of its present owners, Mr. and Mrs. Lucien Guin, Sr.

The original relics of *Monmouth* have been lost to posterity, but the late Mrs. Barnum had furnished it with beautiful pieces of her own family heirlooms. The house has been restored completely, inside and out, and once again takes its place as a landmark in Mississippi history.

PLATE XXV *MONMOUTH*

THE BURN

1832

The Burn was built for Mr. John P. Walworth, an early settler from Ohio en route to New Orleans. He was so entranced with Natchez that he remained here to make his fortune. In 1832 he brought skilled workmen into Natchez from the eastern states to erect his house.

The Burn can be referred to as the transition house of Old Natchez. This house left behind the Georgian architectural influence and started the trend toward Greek Revival.

The name, *"The Burn,"* is of Scottish origin and means "The Brook." Formerly a brook ran at the rear of the grounds. When the house was built, its grounds occupied a large acreage, but all of that has gone to make up the blocks of Natchez, for after 138 years *The Burn* is in the heart of the City. The remaining four acres slope gradually away from this white frame house on all sides. Originally *The Burn* was a two full stories, but an early fire destroyed part of the upper floor, and it was rebuilt into a story and a half.

One enters from a curved drive and up sweeping brick steps. The porch is enclosed with banisters connected to four fluted Grecian columns that support the roof. A heavy paneled door is framed with overhead and side lights of old glass set in rectangular shapes, with classic pilasters on the side. A large hall runs the length of the house. In this hall is the most outstanding architectural feature of *The Burn*, which is a semi-suspended spiral staircase that has the original cypress treds. The handrail is of carved mahogany. Floors are of six inch wide cypress boards, typical of that found in houses built in this period. The interior is much more spacious than one would assume, having four rooms on the main floor as well as four bedrooms and a sitting room upstairs. The basement has been converted into a large recreation area. To the

rear and side is a two story brick building that housed the old kitchen and servants' quarters.

During the Civil War, Major Douglas Walworth, C.S.A., had come to his father's home on sick leave. While here, a courier was dispatched to inform the major that a Federal landing party from the Union gunboat Essex was about to invade the city. The Silver Grays, which was a unit made up of the elderly male citizens and young boys of the city, was marched toward the landing and ordered to fire on the invaders by Major Walworth. Commander W. D. Porter of the Essex retaliated by shelling the city for one hour, and the Mayor unconditionally surrendered the city. The only casualty in this bombardment was a little seven year old girl, Rosalie Beekman, who was struck by a shell fragment and passed away the following day. The ironical part of this story is that in 1935, Mr. and Mrs. S. Beekman Laub purchased *The Burn* and had it completely restored. The late Mr. Laub was a nephew of Rosalie Beekman, who was the great aunt of Mrs. Cooper, the author's wife. After the city was occupied by Union forces, *The Burn* was used as headquarters by Major John P. Coleman. Later it was used as a hospital for sick and wounded Federal soldiers. During this occupation the large trees were cut and used as firewood. Fortifications were built surrounding the house, as its grounds fell within the compound of Fort McPherson.

While the Laubs resided at *The Burn*, they restored the gardens. There were planted over 125 varieties of camellias, alone, in addition to scores of other plants and shrubs. These are so arranged that in the springtime especially there is a burst of blooms in all directions.

In recent years the property was purchased from the Laub estate by Mr. S. Barnett Serio, Sr., who has maintained *The Burn* much as it was in bygone days.

PLATE XVI *THE BURN*

The Burn as it appeared in 1864 during the
occupation of Natchez by Union Forces.
Note Union Troops standing on steps.
PHOTO FROM THE STEWART COLLECTION

OAKLAND

Circa 1835

Oakland is a lovely plantation-type house whose exterior is marked by simplicity and whose interior combines lavishness with charm.

This house was built by a prominent engineer of early Natchez, Captain Horatio Sprague Eustis, for his wife, Catherine Chotard Eustis. It stands on property that was once a part of the famous Alexander Moore estate, which was reputed to reach from Port Gibson, Mississippi, to Baton Rouge, Louisiana.

The Eustis family resided at *Oakland* until 1857 when it was sold to a cousin of Mrs. Eustis, John Minor. In recent years *Oakland* has become the property of Mr. and Mrs. Lawrence Adams.

Oakland is a sturdy brick house covered with stucco and scored so as to resemble stone. A full gallery extends across the front and has recessed wings on either side. The gallery is traditionally built with railings and wide stairs. The doorway has rectangular overhead lights. Another interesting exterior feature of *Oakland* is its heavy hand-cut storm blinds.

The interior of the house gives a feeling of spaciousness. The ceilings are unusually high, sixteen and one-half feet. The central hall is flanked by rooms on either side closed by tremendous mahogany sliding doors. Windows to the front extend to the floor. This arrangement provides the utmost of ventilation.

The furnishings of Oakland, some of which were in the house originally, represent the period during which it was built. One of the interesting pieces is an enormous armoire located in the master bedroom. It came originally from another of the great houses of Natchez, Homewood.

The present owners have converted the basement into a charming recreation area and living quarters. Also featured here are two cistern rooms, topped by cast iron covers stamped "C. B. Churchhill & Co., Natchez, Miss. 1859." The dependencies to the rear of the house have also been restored as apartments.

In the library hangs a portrait of Gerard Brandon II, the first native-born governor of the State of Mississippi. His son, Gerard III, was the builder of Brandon Hall, one of the other fine houses within a stone's throw of the Natchez Trace. Governor Brandon is the great-great grandfather of Mrs. Adams.

Oakland derives its name from the grounds, for it sits in a spot overshadowed by oaks. As the shadows lengthen beneath the trees, *Oakland* looks mellow and serene — proud of its heritage.

PLATE XXVII *OAKLAND*

Library at Oakland.

Window in basement showing
servant quarters to the rear of Oakland.

Cistern room in basement at Oakland.

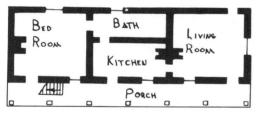

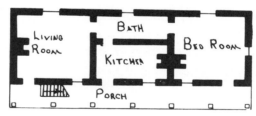

SERVANT QUARTERS

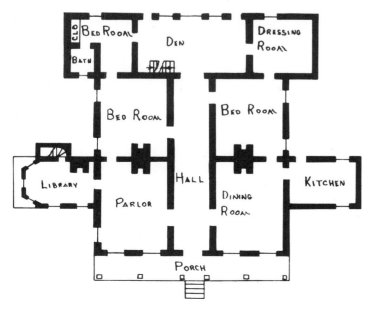

MAIN FLOOR PLAN

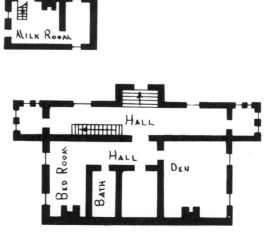

BASEMENT FLOOR PLAN

D'EVEREUX

1840

D'Evereux takes its place proudly among the fine examples of Greek Revival architecture in the United States. A Mr. Hardy designed and built *D'Evereux* for Mr. and Mrs. St. John Elliott in 1840. *D'Evereux* was the scene of one of the most elaborate balls ever held in Natchez. Mr. Henry Clay was a close friend of Mr. Elliott's and while Mr. Clay was seeking the office of President of the United States, this ball was given in his honor.

Mr. and Mrs. Elliott were not blessed with an heir and desiring to have his house retained by a member of his family, Mr. Elliott offered *D'Evereux* to a nephew on condition that he change his name to St. John Elliott. His nephew was satisfied with his own name, so he declined the offer. Mr. Elliott at his death in 1855 willed *D'Evereux* to the Catholic Church to be used as an orphanage after the death of his wife. Mrs. Elliott made arrangements for the church to build an orphanage and retained ownership of her home. *D'Evereux* was unoccupied for a time, until Mrs. Elliott returned and resided there until her death in 1876. She willed *D'Evereux* to her 16 year old niece, Margaret Martin, daughter of General William T. Martin, C.S.A. In 1925, Miss Myra Virginia Smith purchased *D'Evereux* from Mrs. Bayard Shields, nee Margaret Martin. Miss Smith had many needed repairs made to the house and had the undergrowth removed from the once magnificent gardens. During the Civil War, Union soldiers camped on the grounds and destroyed most of the plants and flowers popular at that time.

After the death of Miss Smith in 1961, *D'Evereux* and its furnishings were willed to the University of Chicago. The property was put up for sale and was purchased by Mr. and Mrs. T. B. Buckles and Mr. T. B. Buckles, Jr. in 1962. Immediately after acquiring *D'Evereux*, the Buckles had the house completely restored and its grounds planted with a variety of shrubs and flowers that give a profusion of color in the four seasons of the year. Many of the original pieces of furniture have been obtained and have been restored through the efforts of Mr. and Mrs. T. B. Buckles and Mr. and Mrs. T. B. Buckles, Jr.

The symmetrical beauty of *D'Evereux* is evident with its six fluted and slightly tapered Doric columns which support the entablature, its unusual hipped roof that is topped with a cupola and enclosed with wooden banisters. On approaching the house, one sees a resemblance to a great white Grecian temple. *D'Evereux* is sitting a short distance from the highway, resting among enormous oak and magnolia trees laden with moss. The columns, 3 feet in diameter, are spaced 12 feet apart and fronts a porch 12 feet wide. A small balcony with cast iron banisters is attached over the entrance, a substitute for the usual second storied porch found on many of the other houses of this design.

A three-step mounting block faces three groups of six steps each leading to the porch which extends the width of the house. Mounting blocks are found at many of the houses for this was a means of mounting horses or entering carriages.

A severely simple recessed doorway with rectangular side and overhead lights opens into a hallway that runs the length of the house. At the rear of the hall a door equal in size to that of the front has a gracious fanlight and side lights fretted with straight and carved strips of cypress wood studded with small lead ornaments giving the appearance of leaded glass.

The double parlors, 18 feet by 24 feet, joined by large folding doors have jib windows opening on the front and rear porches. Baseboards in the parlors are painted to resemble the white marble mantels. Two plaster medallions in the center of the ceilings are composed of swirled acanthus leaves (symbol of immortality) radiating from the center and alternating with flower spikes. This is encircled by a band of units of the Greek Key, also a symbol of immortality, alternating with the conventionalized honeysuckle, symbol of hospitality. The border around the walls just below the ceiling repeats the acanthus motif with the flowers, and is bordered with the Egg and Dart motif, symbolizing the beginning and end of life.

The dining room on the left of the hallway balances the front parlor in size and shape. The space behind the dining room is shared by a Jeffersonian stairwell opening off of the hall, with a swing staircase bordered by a slender mahogany handrail, connecting the first and second floors with the attic, paralleled by a service hallway and a most attractive kitchen.

The second floor has four bedrooms opening from the hallway. This floor plan is a duplicate of the one on the first floor. Window cornices, mirrors and furnishings are of the period in which the house was built.

D'Evereux has been returned to its former grandeur and depicts so perfectly the lush years prior to the Civil War.

PLATE XXVIII *D'EVEREUX*

Rear view of D'Evereux.

Front parlor at D'Evereux.

Dining room at D'Evereux.

Privy or outhouse at D'Evereux.

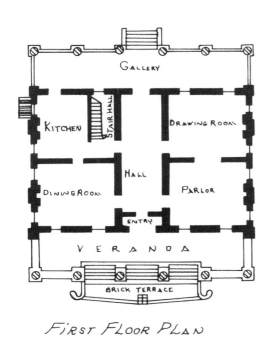

FIRST FLOOR PLAN

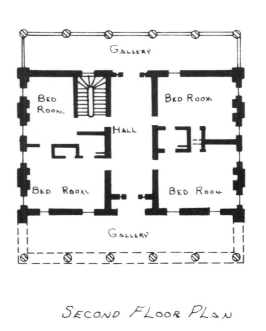

SECOND FLOOR PLAN

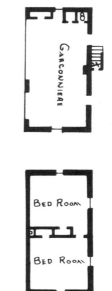

LANSDOWNE

1853

Lansdowne was built in 1853, not too many years before the Civil War, in the opulent period when nearly all the better houses were being erected in Greek Revival. Thus *Lansdowne* is a modified form of this architecture.

Of stuccoed brick, it is one-storied with a basement — of the cottage type. The word, cottage, however, is misleading. The interior of *Lansdowne* is far more spacious than many mansions; and its foundations were strongly built, it is felt that the owners contemplated adding a second story.

Lansdowne was built by the George Marshalls, and descendants of the builder, Mr. and Mrs. George Marshall and Mrs. Singleton Gardner, still own the house. Many of the original furnishings, over 100 years old, remain. It was a lavish home, for George Marshall who was rich in his own right, married Charlotte Hunt, daughter of one of the wealthiest men in Natchez.

Wide steps curve upward to a gallery bordered by fluted columns and iron grillwork. The interior of *Lansdowne* is magnificent. The hall is fifteen feet wide and sixty-five feet long. A parlor to the left has one of the finest mantels in Natchez — white marble carved in calla lily design. Furnishings are in rosewood. The carpet is Aubusson. Door knobs are silver plated. From the parlor, double sliding doors open into a tremendous banquet hall about twenty-five feet square. The silver, china and glassware in this room are elegant.

On the opposite side are the bedrooms, all of which have black Egyptian marble mantels. In the rear of the house is a brick court with two double story buildings forming two sides of the court. These formerly housed the outdoor kitchen, a school room, and employees' rooms. *Lansdowne* was the first house in Natchez to operate its own gas plant and the beautiful chandeliers in the home originally burned gas.

Lansdowne had its share of heartbreak during the Civil War. While Marshall lay ill, Mrs. Marshall was struck down by a Yankee looter who had demanded the keys to her home. She carried forever the mark which followed her haughty refusal.

Some of her fine things were saved through the efforts of a Negro servant who helped to bury them. But some of the pieces of her exquisite apricot colored china were broken into bits and scattered along the road. The remainder of that set can be seen today at *Lansdowne*.

Surrounded by all these heirlooms, one thinks with nostalgia of what life at *Lansdowne* must have been like in the glorious days before the Civil War.

Mrs. George M. Marshall is the author of *Six Little Girls of Lansdowne* which is a story of her granddaughters and their activities living on a cotton plantation.

PLATE XXIX *LANSDOWNE*

Dining room at Lansdowne.

Privy or outhouse at Lansdowne.

One of the matching outer buildings. This one was the kitchen and servant quarters at Lansdowne.

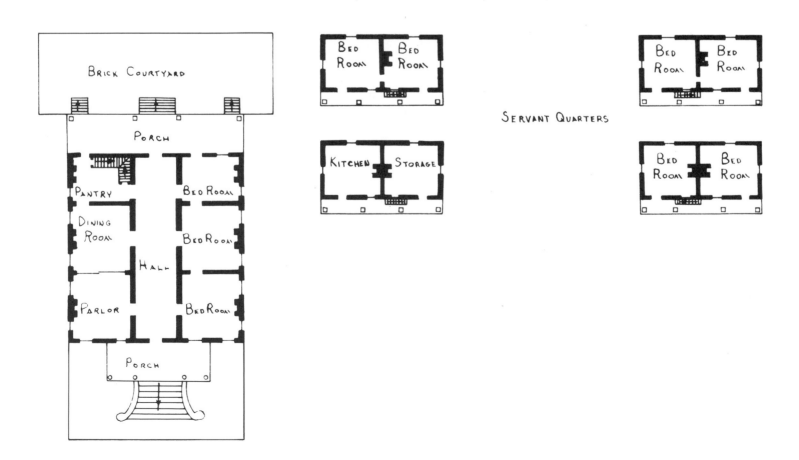

SERVANT QUARTERS

THE BRIERS

1812

This house in its semi-tropical and secluded setting can lay claim to being one of the most historically important dwellings within the State of Mississippi. It was here that Jefferson Davis, who became President of the Confederate States of America, married the Natchez belle, Varina Howell.

It is thought that *The Briers* was built for Mr. Arthur Mahan in 1812. Records indicate that the house was occupied by the Mahan family for only six years. The property was purchased by Mr. John Perkins in 1818 and changed ownership again in the early 1820's with the acquisition of the property by Mr. William Burr Howell.

It is easy to see why Mr. Mahan had his house constructed on this site. To reach *The Briers*, one must follow a narrow winding road overlaced by tall trees and creeping vines and across gorges, or bayous, as they are called in Mississippi. On drawing nearer it is evident that the land slopes gently away from the house. The house overlooks the Mississippi River from a bluff several hundred feet high. From this bluff is a breath-taking panoramic view of the River and the lowlands of Louisiana.

The Briers is a typical example of a Mississippi planter's house of the early 1800's. It is a white frame house having one and one-half stories and a large basement. This house is without the lavishness of many of the other houses built in Natchez in the latter part of the nineteenth century. A wide gallery runs the width of the house and is enclosed with banisters connected to ten small tapered columns which support the steeply sloped roof. Four dormer windows protrude from the roof which gives the necessary balance to this house. There are three entrance doorways leading from the gallery, all of which have beautiful fanlights above. The main doorway is in the center of the house which opens into a hall that is unusual as it has a rounded ceiling such as found in many of the early Spanish buildings. The overall floor plan follows the pattern found in many of the other houses of this period with a central hall and large rooms on either side.

To the right of this hall is the parlor where on Febru-
ary 26, 1845, the marriage vows were taken by Mr. Davis and Miss Howell, before members of the Howell and Davis families. The ceremony was conducted by Reverend David Page, Rector of the Trinity Episcopal Church of Natchez. After the wedding, Mr. Davis and his bride left Natchez and visited at Woodville, Mississippi, Bayou Sara and New Orleans, Louisiana. After this honeymoon trip, the couple went to Brierfield, the plantation home of Mr. Davis, located on the bank of the Mississippi River, a short distance south of Vicksburg, Mississippi.

To the rear of the central hallway is a large sun parlor. In this room are five Moorish styled arches and the back wall consists of nine windows which were added in recent years to afford more comfort. Twin staircases with mahogany handrails are at either end, ascending to the upper floor. The upstairs contains four rooms, two of which are unusually large and are connected with folding doors. The doors can be folded back so that this area can be converted into a banquet hall. It was here that the wedding breakfast for Jefferson Davis and his bride was held.

During the Civil War, *The Briers* was not disturbed by the invading Union Army as were many of the other houses located near the bluff. In the tragic years of 1861 to 1865, the house was owned and occupied by the Walter Irvine family. During the occupation of Natchez by Union forces, Mrs. Irvine extended several acts of kindness to the soldiers and gained their respect and protection.

After the war clouds cleared, *The Briers* began to deteriorate and it was not until 1927 that it was purchased by Mr. and Mrs. William Winans Wall. The house was in a sad state of repair and much work was required to make it habitable. However, Mr. and Mrs. Wall followed the original plan in their restoration and selected furnishings typical of those used when the house was occupied by the Howell family.

Recently *The Briers* was purchased by the Charisima Corporation. Under the new ownership the house will be refurnished with period pieces which will depict the era in which it was built.

PLATE XXX *THE BRIERS*

121

Parlor at The Briers. In this room was where Jefferson Davis and
Varina Howell were married in 1845.

Dining room at The Briers.

Doorway with fanlight
at The Briers.

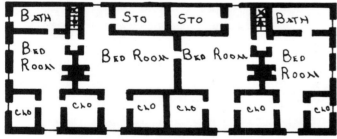

SECOND FLOOR PLAN

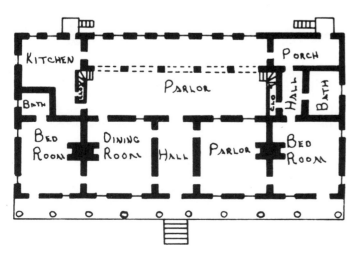

FIRST FLOOR PLAN

RICHMOND

1770-1832-1860

It sometimes happens that a man will do something against all the rules set down by other men — and the result will be an achievement that falls back into the realm of regulations. Such an achievement is *Richmond*, the house that is really three houses, and has become one.

To understand *Richmond*, we must try to visualize it as it was in 1784, when only its central part existed. It must have been a luxurious house for its time . . . its stairway running from the ground to the second floor . . . and its iron banisters. This portion of Richmond has often been called of Spanish architecture, but later designers believe that its design is French, since it is similar to houses in the Teche country of Louisiana. To bear this out, papers hint that it was probably rebuilt from a simple structure already standing, by John St. Germain, a French settler of early Natchez.

This portion of the house has always been called the most interesting part. It has, on its second floor (which throughout the house is the main floor) a double dining room, a hall and two bedrooms. The double dining room is unique, and was probably built because of the French custom of the time of serving one course in one dining room, and then having guests go to the other dining room for the next course.

The floors contain the original solid hand-hewn cypress, and are particularly engaging because the wood is of varying sizes. The lower, or basement, floor has been converted into a play room. It has the original brick paved floor and large brick fireplaces. In earlier days this part of the basement, along with the basement under the remainder of the house, was used for offices and school rooms.

The second part of the house was built by Levin R. Marshall, well-known Natchez banker, after he acquired the house in 1832. This addition took five years to build. It was attached to the side of the French section, and was built in Greek Revival, typical of the architecture of that period. This is now the front of the house. It has a gallery with large Grecian columns, and severe Grecian lines; but Levin Marshall added a Creole flavor when he placed beautiful iron balconies on each austere window.

The Grecian part of the house has a tremendous hall, large double parlors, and two bedrooms on the main (or second) floor; two bedrooms on the third floor, and a number of rooms in the basement. The parlors and the hall are extremely ornate, with beautiful wood carvings, stately pilasters, and elaborate cornices. The parlors are connected with double folding doors, and have the black marble mantels so much in vogue at that time.

In one parlor is the now-famous grand piano used to accompany Jenny Lind when she sang in Natchez in 1851. The story is that the singer arrived for a concert in Natchez in February by boat, and that because of the ice on the hill, her own piano could not be moved from the boat to the hall in which she was to sing. Therefore the piano at *Richmond* was used.

The final part of *Richmond* was added to the rear in 1860, not long before the shot was fired at Fort Sumter. It is a typical colonial brick building, and now is composed of bedrooms.

Richmond, complete, has forty rooms. It has been in the hands of the Marshalls since 1832, and the fifth and sixth generations of the Marshall family now reside there.

PLATE XXXI   *RICHMOND*

Grand piano used to accompany Jenny Lind, located in front parlor at Richmond.

Main hall and stairway at Richmond.

Side view of Richmond showing each section, from left, 1832 - 1770 - 1860.

Portrait of Levin R. Marshall
at Richmond.

Infant's teaster bed at Richmond.

ROSALIE

1820

Probably the most historic spot in Natchez is occupied by *Rosalie*, the beautiful house owned by the Mississippi Society, Daughters of the American Revolution; for it was near this site that the French first built Fort Rosalie in 1716, named for the Duchess de Pontchartrain. It was here that the French, the British, then the Spanish, and finally the Americans raised their successive flags over the Natchez Territory.

The house itself, a solid Georgian mansion, was built by Peter Little, who had amassed a fortune in the lumber business in Natchez. It was he who owned and operated the first sawmill in this territory. There is a beguiling story about Peter Little and his young wife, who was his ward, but it will be told in the story of The Parsonage, another lovely house not far from *Rosalie*.

Rosalie took seven years to build. It was designed by James S. Griffin, of Baltimore, the brother-in-law of Little. Griffin designed many of the fine houses in and around Natchez. *Rosalie* is of red brick, with double galleries and large white columns about half way across the center of the exterior. With Arlington and Gloucester, this house has been called the finest example of Georgian in Natchez. As in the other houses, the ceilings of *Rosalie* were raised high to take care of the hot Southern summers.

The interior of *Rosalie* follows the regular pattern — a wide center hallway on both lower and upper floors, and large rooms on either side. Downstairs, double parlors to the left have white carved mantels of handsome design. Over the mantels are identical gold leaf French mirrors. While the Federal troops were approaching Natchez, the owners of Rosalie and their servants busied themselves by wrapping these huge mirrors in blankets, and storing them in the Fort Rosalie hillside behind the house, where they remained until after the war. Other furnishings were also buried, including brass fenders and fireplace sets, which were hidden in the stable yard, and lost sight of until unearthed many years later by children digging in the dirt.

For all the activity to hide the valuables, *Rosalie* was spared the sad fate that overtook many of the other houses during the war, although it was occupied by Union General Walter Q. Gresham and his officers. Thus *Rosalie* still has many of its original furnishings. In the double parlors are beautiful carpets, two antique pianos and two complete parlor sets, made to order for these rooms by the famous craftsman, Belter.

To the right of the hall are the library and banquet room. One of *Rosalie's* prized possessions is a set of Sèvres, old Paris china, with no two pieces alike. The china has a deep green border, and is the same period as the original china, which is no longer at *Rosalie*. The D. A. R., in restoring the house, has added draperies and other furnishings in keeping with the times.

Rosalie is really four stories, with its basement and attic. A mahogany recessed circular stairway leads up from the first floor to the attic.

During the Union occupation, General Gresham, the commanding officer, occupied *Rosalie*, and his wife came from the North to join him. The owners were Mr. and Mrs. Andrew L. Wilson. Mr. Wilson was away, but Mrs. Wilson was allowed to remain in her home until it was discovered that she was a leading force in a Confederate underground. She was banished to Atlanta, where she stayed until the close of the war. However, she and the Greshams remained fast friends, and the Greshams visited the Wilsons after the war and occupation took over.

General Grant spent three days at *Rosalie*. The bed in which he slept can still be seen by visitors to this house.

The Mississippi Society, Daughters of the American Revolution, purchased *Rosalie* in 1938. Much credit must be given these ladies for the restoration of a famous landmark and the beautification of its gardens.

PLATE XXXII *ROSALIE*

129

Double parlor at Rosalie.

Rear view of Rosalie.

Arabesque in front parlor at Rosalie.

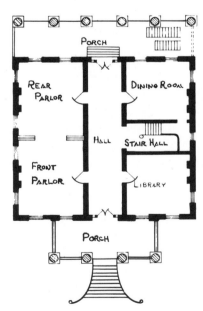

FIRST FLOOR PLAN

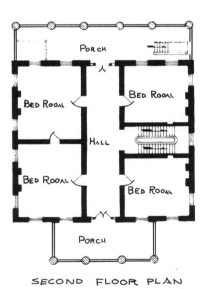

SECOND FLOOR PLAN

131

THE PARSONAGE

1840

There is one house in Natchez whose history carries with it the touch of whimsy that reveals to us that the people who built these houses were not a series of names and dates, but actual human beings.

That home is *The Parsonage*; and this is its story. Peter Little, an early successful sawmill operator and property owner, had married Eliza Low, a woman much younger than himself, and for her had built Rosalie, whose history you have already read.

As Eliza Little grew older, she also grew deeply religious; and it became her custom to entertain traveling ministers constantly in her home. Her husband, desiring some privacy in his home, offered to build a place to house the visiting ministers and *The Parsonage* is the result.

It was completed in 1840, a sturdy mansion not far from the Little home, Rosalie. It occupies part of what was once the old Spanish parade grounds high on the bluffs overlooking the Mississippi River, and from its gallery one can face the sun setting over the river.

The Parsonage is a solid house built to endure, of the very finest materials. Recently the paint was removed from the brick and the original appearance of the house was restored. It has a basement, a first floor and an attic. Steps rise high over the basement to the front gallery, which is very roomy.

From the gallery one enters a square reception hall, to the left of which is the parlor. *The Parsonage* has some elegant furnishings, many of which are seen in this room. One outstanding piece is a marble shelved étagère with mirrored back. Among the china on this is a teapot which made the trip to Natchez from Kentucky more than a century and a half ago. Over the parlor mantel is a huge gold leaf mirror. Gracing the mantel are three bronze whale-oil lamps with crystal globes and pendants.

The dining room is behind the parlor, and between them are sliding doors. Furniture here is of walnut, and the silver and china are outstanding. An interesting painting is in the dining room. In the early days traveling painters already had paintings of background and bodies, and all that was necessary was to dub in the features of the subject. The painting at *The Parsonage* is of this type of one of the early owners.

This room has about 200 pieces of Sèvres china in the Rose Pompadour design, with no two pieces identical.

The bedrooms are also beautifully furnished with pieces dating back many years. At least two pieces, both chests, go back to 1780. The house has a bedroom ell added about 1878, and an unusual recessed back porch. The basement was originally used for a kitchen and servants' quarters, but it has been transformed into a most useful living quarters possessing a charm of its own.

Present owners are Mr. and Mrs. Orrick Metcalfe. Five generations of the Metcalfe family have resided at *The Parsonage*.

PLATE XXIII *THE PARSONAGE*

Breakfast room located in basement at The Parsonage.

Spiral post bed in basement
of The Parsonage.

Plantation made cabinet located in basement at The Parsonage.

Quaint stairway leading to the second floor at The Parsonage.

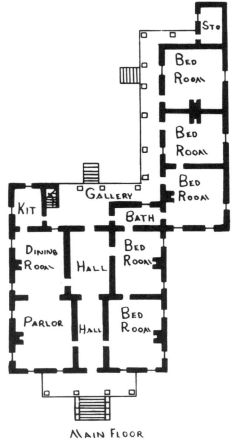

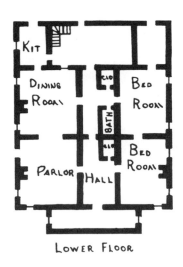

STO

BED ROOM

BED ROOM

BED ROOM

GALLERY

KIT

BATH

DINING ROOM

HALL

BED ROOM

PARLOR

HALL

BED ROOM

MAIN FLOOR

KIT

DINING ROOM

BED ROOM

BATH

PARLOR

HALL

BED ROOM

LOWER FLOOR

BONTURA or EVANSVIEW

1790-1830

Bontura stands on the historic bluff site of the original village of French colonists of 1720.

During the later British and Spanish regimes, this was the center of the Village Green or Public Common belonging to the Fort. Old records, maps, drawings and statements show that the house was originally built by a Spanish official before 1790, and was standing much as it is today in the 1830's.

This is one of the most intriguing of all Natchez houses. A glance at the accompanying photograph shows that it belongs, perhaps, more to New Orleans than to Natchez — and perhaps even more to the Romantic countries of Europe. It is flush with the street, with its lacy grilled galleries. The house stretches long and narrow until the rear wing makes an ell with the front, and forms a picturesque courtyard. *Bontura* is like nothing else in Natchez.

This house was purchased in 1860 by a Portuguese man who had made a fortune in Natchez and in Natchez-Under-the-Hill, Josef Bontura. Bontura enlarged the house and added to its Creole savor by his style of living and hospitality.

The lines of the two-and-one-half-storied front are severe, broken by double grilled galleries and one dormer window, like an eye looking out upon the Mississippi River and the Louisiana country beyond.

The front door opens into a small hallway, to the right of which is the parlor. Focal point of this room is the fireplace, with its simple mantel. Mr. and Mrs. Hugh Evans have completely restored the house, and the authentic pieces in the parlor, as well as in the entire house, enhance the Old World atmosphere.

The dining room just behind the parlor extends the entire width of the building. It has fireplaces on either end, as do many of the larger rooms of that period. This room has a triple-hung window which looks out on the courtyard, and a door which opens on a covered brick terrace. Elegant Sheffield silver and china pieces are in the dining room.

Bontura also has a large ball room, which was probably used as a music room and banquet hall on various occasions. Behind the ballroom is the library, with a beautiful early handmade cypress mantel.

The upper floor has a number of bedrooms, all of which are furnished in appropriate style. The airy upper galleries give a particularly splendid view of the river.

At *Bontura* is a basement, the early use of which has set imaginations to working. At one time there was a specific law against basements that required moving of dirt — and although one deed specifically forbids building of any basement — the basement is there, twenty feet square and nine feet high. Relics of interesting brick work below the floor have inspired legends of hidden treasure or ancient wine casks.

The courtyard at *Bontura* is enclosed on three sides — on two sides by the house itself, and on the third side by a tall brick wall. A fence of iron grillwork separates it from the street, from which it is visible. Lovely trees and shrubbery have made it one of the garden spots of Natchez. The five enormous arches of the coach house open into the courtyard and side street in the Vieux Carré manner.

Bontura was one of the houses damaged when the Naval ship, USS Essex, fired on Natchez during the Civil War. A shell exploded against the side wall. Even though *Bontura* literally felt the pangs of war and the years that followed were not so kind to this as to other houses, once again it presents the charm of yesteryear.

Mr. and Mrs. Hugh H. Evans donated *Bontura* to the Mississippi Chapter of the National Society of Colonial Dames of America. It was with this gift that the name was changed to Evansview.

PLATE XXXIV *BONTURA or EVANSVIEW*

Dining room at Bontura. Here hangs the early painting
of "The River Front at Natchez," by Sarah Dorsey.

Lovely brick arches at Bontura.

Ante-bellum child's play things at Bontura.

View of side and front
of wing at Bontura.

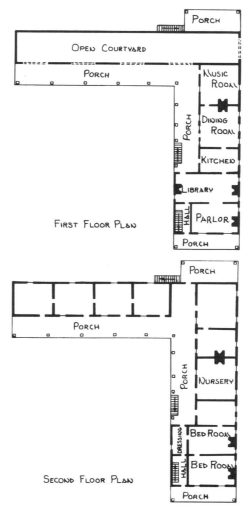

FIRST FLOOR PLAN

SECOND FLOOR PLAN

COTTAGE GARDENS

1793

With the purchase of *Cottage Gardens* by Mr. and Mrs. William Carl McGehee in 1963 began one of the most elaborate restorations undertaken in Natchez. The finest materials that could be obtained were used. Much of the building material used was as old as the house. Several shipments of assorted materials arrived from New Orleans, Louisiana, and other points that could supply the needed items.

Cottage Gardens stands on land granted Don Jose Vidal by the Spanish Crown in 1793. Vidal was a captain in the Spanish Army attached to the Post of Natchez. In 1798, he was acting Spanish Governor of Natchez. While he was residing at *Cottage Gardens*, his wife, Donna, was taken by death. At this time Vidal's duties carried him across the Mississippi River to what is now the town of Vidalia, Louisiana. For the love of his Donna, he had her tomb built upon the high bluff overlooking the river. While attending to the affairs of Post Concord, he could view her tomb from his headquarters. After the death of Don Jose Vidal, *Cottage Gardens* was owned by several different families. Many years ago the house became the property of Mr. A. H. Foster. Members of his family occupied the house until it was sold to Mr. and Mrs. McGehee.

During the Civil War the lovely gardens were destroyed as Union soldiers camped on the grounds. This house fell within the Union Army compound of Fort McPherson. Horses were permitted to trample through the gardens of all of the houses that were within the Fort.

There were several changes made in restoring *Cottage Gardens*. One of which was the erection of a brick wing to replace the original kitchen that had deteriorated so that it was beyond restoration. This change has enhanced the overall appearance and has provided for the insertion of modern appliances. This wing contains a most attractive breakfast room. The walls are of natural brick and exposed cypress beams in the ceiling and floored with cobblestones from New Orleans. The kitchen is panelled with pickled cypress boards with the same detail carried forward in the ceiling and floors. In the hallway adjacent to the kitchen, there is a stairway that descends to the basement. This area has been remodeled and is now used for recreation. This floor contains guest bedrooms and modern baths.

The main floor of the house has a central hall. To the left of the hall is the parlor and to the rear is the dining room. To the right of the hall is the library, which has been decorated in a complete Georgian motif. To the rear of this room is a spacious bedroom. Two of the noted features of *Cottage Gardens* are the lovely semi-spiral staircase located midway in the central hall and the beautiful fanlighted doorways at the front and rear of the hall. A duplicate of this fanlight separates the parlor from the dining room.

The second floor has been remodeled in a manner which is most attractive and convenient, containing three bedrooms, large dressing rooms and modern baths.

The once over-grown gardens have been cleared and a formal pattern has been restored. Within a few years, the gardens will also be one of the outstanding features of *Cottage Gardens*.

Mr. and Mrs. McGehee are collecting early period pieces of furniture which will depict the era in which the house was built. The overall appearance that Mr. and Mrs. McGehee have attained is a beautiful house made most livable.

PLATE XXXV *COTTAGE GARDENS*

Cottage Gardens — North side of house
in the first stage of restoration.

PHOTO COURTESY MR. AND MRS. WILLIAM CARL McGEHEE

Cottage Gardens — Entrance hall with
semi-spiral stairway and fanlighted
doorways.

Cottage Gardens — Breakfast room located in kitchen wing.

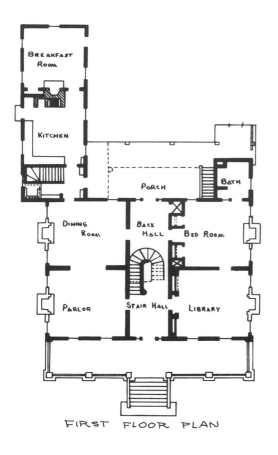

FIRST FLOOR PLAN

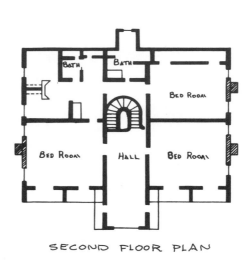

SECOND FLOOR PLAN

WHITE WINGS

1833-1854

White Wings stands upon a town lot that was granted to Mr. James Moore by the Spanish Government in 1795. This grant was signed by the Spanish Governor of Natchez, Don Manuel Gayosa de Lemos, on the 18th day of January in 1795. Mr. Moore was a merchant who operated a business establishment in the Natchez-Under-the-Hill. Records indicate that some type of residence was built upon this lot for Mr. Moore in 1796.

In 1811, the property was sold for $600.00 to Mr. John S. Miller. After the death of Mr. Miller in 1824, the property was sold for a smaller amount than it brought in the sale of 1811; therefore, something must have destroyed the house that was built here. In 1833, Mrs. Sarah Robinson purchased the lot and must have had a house constructed on this site. It is believed that the present *White Wings* was built around the house that was constructed for Mrs. Robinson. Mr. Charles Meeks, one of the early bankers of Natchez, purchased the property in 1854. Mr. Meeks had the house enlarged and through this work created the present appearance of *White Wings*.

White Wings is a rambling frame cottage with a variety of architectural patterns. Its floors are of random width cypress boards such as is found in many of the early houses of this section. An unusual feature found in this house by workmen some years ago is one roof built above another. When the additions were built, a new roof was constructed above the existing one.

The property was acquired by the Honorable and Mrs. John R. Junkin in 1929. Furnishings of the period in which the house was built were placed within its rooms. Under this ownership, the house has been kept in excellent repair. The lawn is beautifully maintained and is shaded by large magnolia trees and flowering shrubs native to this region. The Honorable John R. Junkin has devoted much of his life to the political activity of the State and is now Speaker of the House of Representatives of the State of Mississippi.

144

PLATE XXXVI *WHITE WINGS*

LINDEN

1785-1818-1840

The influence of *Linden* has been felt in architectural circles for many years. The original section was thought to have been built around 1785, but the builder and designer are unknown.

The original portion of *Linden*, which is now the center, is two stories, put together with wooden pegs, and has two rooms on each floor with a hall in the middle. The house is built of solid cypress. This section has beautiful hand carvings in cypress over the doors, by the windows, and on the stairway.

Until recently, this part of the house also had marble mantels. However, Mr. and Mrs. Frank Fauntleroy, present owners, knew that in the period when this house was built, marble mantels were not in use. Mrs. Fauntleroy conducted a search throughout the house and uncovered the original cypress mantels, hand-carved to match the other carving in the house. This was indeed a find.

These mantels had eight coats of paint on them; and in removing coat by coat, she came across a black stratum on the next to the last layer. It is recalled that in 1799, the year of the death of George Washington, many things were painted black.

When the house was acquired by U. S. Senator Thomas Reed in 1818, he added to the width, making the house 98 feet across. He built a lovely gallery across the entire front, and on the center portion constructed a two-storied gallery. It is also believed he added the front door which, as the photograph shows, is one of the outstanding fan-lighted doors in this section, and is said to have been influenced by the Grecian mode then coming in vogue.

Mrs. Fauntleroy's great-great-grandmother acquired the house in 1840 and added on a brick wing and a frame wing, to form ells with the main house, to take care of her thirteen children. The brick wing has posts of solid cedar, hand hewn from giant cedar trees, and set in place with wooden pegs. It housed a kitchen, store rooms and school rooms.

The parlor of *Linden* is outstanding . . . much of the furnishings having been purchased by Mrs. Fauntleroy's great-great-grandmother. At that time Victorian and Empire were stylish, and the furnishings reflect this trend.

The dining room has a cypress punkah, painted white. In this room are also three of the earliest prints of Audubon's work, the oldest having been made in 1833. A set of china, Old Paris, has nearly 400 pieces and was made in 1810.

Six generations of the same family have lived at *Linden*. The house rises from the top of a gentle slope and, set behind mossy oaks, with its low rambling lines, is the essence of Southern homes.

PLATE XXXVII *LINDEN*

Outstanding doorway at Linden.

Dining room with punkah at Linden.

1. DINING ROOM
2. LIVING ROOM
3. BED ROOM
4. KITCHEN
5. STORAGE
6. BATH
7. PARLOR
8. BREAKFAST ROOM
9. PORCH
10. COURT YARD

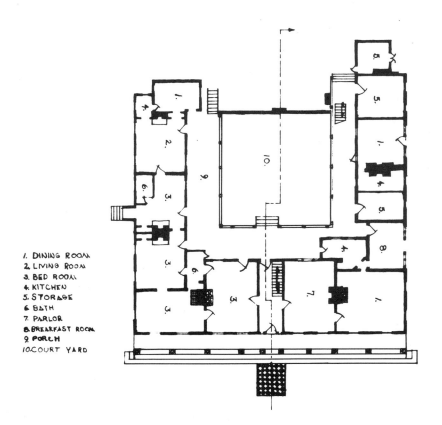

FIRST FLOOR PLAN

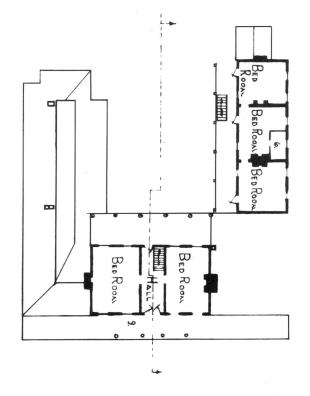

SECOND FLOOR PLAN

149

AIRLIE

1790

Airlie is an example of a house that grew, by the addition of several wings, to a lovely Southern home embodying hospitality and comfort.

The main portion was built prior to 1790, during the time of the Spanish occupancy, and is believed by some to be the oldest house in Natchez. Later owners added wings, as the need arose, at various elevations, giving the interior a charm of its own.

The wings were added to the width of the house and because of its tremendous breadth, *Airlie* is difficult to photograph. While it has no particular style of architecture, it can simply be called early Natchez, with its wide front steps leading to a gallery of large proportions.

It is believed that the main portion was built by some early Spanish official. However, during the ante-bellum days *Airlie* was known as the Buckner home, because it became the property of Aylette Buckner, a prominent lawyer, and great-grandfather of the present owners, the Ayres P. Merrill family.

Airlie has long figured in the early history of Natchez. During the Civil War, when the Union gunboats were anchored in the Mississippi River at Natchez, *Airlie* was used as a hospital for the Union soldiers.

Mellowed by the years, this old house has been carefully restored without impairing the charm of its original architecture. Rough-hewn beams, mortised together, old fireplaces, many small-paned windows, handmade blinds and other features attest to the skill and patience of its early builders.

In the long low-ceilinged dining room hang a number of portraits by artists of note. Also of interest is the handsome family silver service, a rare tea-set of Old English china and a dinner set of Rose DuBarry.

Because *Airlie* has remained in possession of the descendants of its early owners, it is furnished throughout with exquisite heirloom pieces of mahogany and rosewood, and retains an atmosphere of the days of long ago.

PLATE XXXVIII   *AIRLIE*

Parlor at Airlie.

Front entrance
at Airlie.

152

Marble topped serving table at Airlie.

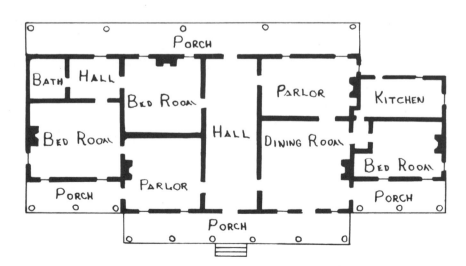

AUBURN

1812

In the heart of Duncan Park, within sound of the merry voices of hundreds of Natchez children, is one of the most magnificent mansions of all — *Auburn*, which was given to the City of Natchez for the "amusement, entertainment and recreation without cost or monetary consideration, of Natchez citizens."

Auburn is built of red brick, burned by slaves on the grounds. It is two-storied, with wide double galleries supported by four massive white columns. Although all of *Auburn* is lovely, perhaps two of its features have created more enthusiasm than any other.

One is its front doorway — a specimen of classic perfection. Beautiful carved woods form overhead and side lights, which are made into unusual geometric patterns.

The second exciting feature is *Auburn's* spiral stairway from its first to its second floor. This stairway is perfectly balanced and completely unsupported. It has been viewed by interested architects from all parts of the United States.

Auburn has a tremendous hallway through the center of the house, and opening from the hall, spacious parlors, two dining rooms — a large one and a small one, a library and smoking room. Upstairs are six giant bedrooms.

It has one of the most extensive of outdoor buildings, including former servants' quarters, kitchen, milk house, and other features. The mansion was built in 1812 by the architect, Levi Weeks. About 1815 it was purchased from the Lyman Harding Estate by Dr. Stephen Duncan, who moved to Natchez from Pennsylvania seven years before, and had become immensely wealthy.

Dr. Duncan became president of Mississippi's first bank, which he helped organize. He is said to have owned five hundred slaves. Among the many guests at *Auburn* were Edward Everett Hale and Henry Clay.

Dr. Duncan's lavish life ended — a sacrifice to a cause. He became involved as far as the Mississippi Supreme Court and the Mississippi Legislature in his efforts to have a dead friend's slaves freed; and during the Civil War, with his heart on the Union side, he finally went to the North, where he died.

In 1911 his heirs deeded the property to the City of Natchez. And now, on the once sloping parkways of a tremendous estate, is one of the most well-equipped children's parks in the South. Here youngsters of all ages may play tennis, softball, baseball and golf; they may swim, ride merry-go-rounds, have birthday parties, dances and outdoor barbecues . . . and even camp out.

PLATE XXXIX   *AUBURN*

The unsupported spiral stairway and Deborah and Carolyn,
the daughters of the author, at Auburn.

Beautiful doorway at Auburn.

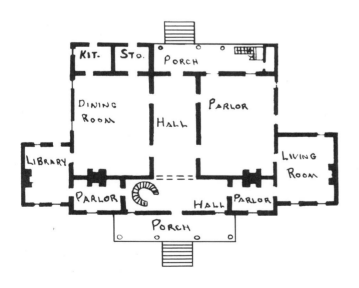

FIRST FLOOR PLAN

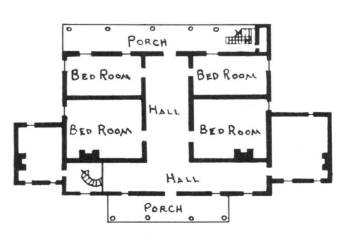

SECOND FLOOR PLAN

THE WIGWAM

Circa 1790

The actual date of the building of *The Wigwam* is not known but from the architectural design and the crudeness of workmanship, it has been established that it is one of the early houses of Natchez. Originally *The Wigwam* was rather a simple house which faced Myrtle Avenue. With several alterations, the front of the house was made to face Oak Street. The last major change altered the entire architectural form of this house.

With a large room constructed to each side and projected forward, it has given it the appearance of having two wings. With this alteration, it recessed the porch and a laced pattern of ironwork was attached which has changed the architectural pattern to French Renaissance. *The Wigwam* is one of the few houses in the Natchez area to possess this architectural form.

It is believed that the major change executed on this house was done under the supervision of Mr. Peter Little, the builder of Rosalie and The Parsonage. As Mr. Little and his wife had no children, they took a niece of Mr. Little's and raised her as their foster child. Her marriage to Douglas L. Rivers was solemnized at Rosalie in 1838. After the young couple returned from their honeymoon, they made *The Wigwam* their home.

There is a story that has been told of a young woman who has been seen coming down the stairs dragging chains behind her. When she alighted from the stairs, she would disappear. It is said that at one time a young woman was confined to her room on the second floor during spells of violence. The upper windows on the Oak Street side were said to have been barred. As with most stories of this type, the woman was supposed to have been seen several times at night.

With the beginning of the Civil War, *The Wigwam* saw many other owners. Finally the house was purchased in 1960 by Dr. Harold C. Hawkins and Mr. H. Hal Garner. Under their direction and with their own skill was begun a slow but artistic restoration. With the efforts of these two young men, *The Wigwam* was retrieved from falling into oblivion. Their interesting restoration can be classified as superb. Through a transfer of property, Mr. and Mrs. L. A. White exchanged their house, Brandon Hall, for *The Wigwam*. The Whites have enhanced *The Wigwam* through their careful selection of rare pieces of furniture and outstanding objects of art. Mr. and Mrs. White now reside in this, one of the most unique houses to be found in Natchez.

PLATE XL *THE WIGWAM*

Main hallway at
The Wigwam.

Wrought iron trim at The Wigwam.

Interior doorway
at The Wigwam.

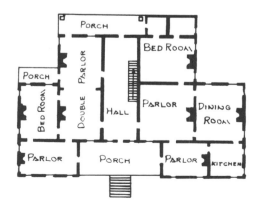

MONTEIGNE

1855

Monteigne is one of the most impressive houses in the South, with its Romanesque columns and wrought iron balustrades and its soft shade of salmon pink stucco. Sitting in the center of a well clipped lawn and shaded by moss hung oak trees over a century old, this house is built of brick which were burned on the place. It has withstood the elements and time as well as the invader.

Monteigne was built for William T. Martin who had come with his family from Kentucky and settled in Vicksburg, Mississippi. Mr. Martin, in search of a career, boarded a steamboat bound for New Orleans. En route the steamboat docked at Natchez. Mr. Martin, desiring to see some of the City, left the boat and went upon the bluff where he met Mr. John P. Walworth. In detecting outstanding qualities possessed by Mr. Martin, Mr. Walworth insisted that he stay in Natchez and study law under him. While studying law, he was employed as schoolmaster for the Walworth children. His interest in the political field is evident, as he was elected district attorney at the age of twenty-two. In 1845, he married into the affluent William C. Conner family. While *Monteigne* was under construction, Mr. and Mrs. Martin made their home at Belmont, one of the other fine houses a short distance out of Natchez. Upon completion of *Monteigne,* Mr. and Mrs. Martin moved in and began the task of beautifying its grounds. The name *Monteigne* was chosen for this house because it was the French Huguenot name of Mr. Martin's ancestors.

Some five years after the completion of *Monteigne,* the war clouds were gathering rapidly. Mr. Martin was not in favor of the State of Mississippi's secession from the Union, but when his adopted State did secede, he was elected Captain of the Adams Troop and commissioned to purchase arms and supplies for his company. After war broke out, Captain Martin was recognized as having great military ability. He rose in rank from Captain to Major General and served under the command of the famous Confederate cavalry leader, General J. E. B. Stuart. Later he served with General Joe Wheeler's command in Tennessee.

When Natchez fell to Union forces, *Monteigne* was a prime target of pillage. For his loyalty to his State and the South, his beloved *Monteigne* suffered severely at the hands of the invaders. Horses were stabled in the drawing room. The house was thrown into shambles; chandeliers were smashed, fine furniture was broken up and used for fire wood. With this unjust intrusion, many scars were inflicted upon *Monteigne.* Its lovely gardens were trampled and laid waste.

After the war, General Martin returned to *Monteigne* and the momentous task of recouping what he could of his lost fortune. Resuming his law practice which was limited for a time and with the means at hand, he undertook the job of repairing his home and restoring its gardens. In the trying times of the reconstruction period which followed the war, General Martin won acclaim and the respect of the people of Mississippi through his sound reasoning and understanding.

In 1928, *Monteigne* was acquired by the Carpenter family. Under their direction, a restoration plan was instituted which included some minor changes. This work helped return *Monteigne* to its former grandeur.

Monteigne was purchased by the William Kendall family in 1935. The present owner, Mrs. Hunter Goodrich, formerly Mrs. William Kendall, recalls a visit that she made to this house while the Carpenter restoration was underway. The floors were being replaced in the drawing room because they were marred by the prints of horse shoes which were imbedded in the wood. Upon the occupancy of *Monteigne* by the Kendall family, in its rooms were placed some of the finest eighteenth century furniture to be found in Natchez. The late Mr. William Kendall was recognized for his knowledge of horticulture, having supervised the cultivation of some three hundred and fifty varieties of camellias and japonicas.

Monteigne is now occupied by Mr. and Mrs. Hunter Goodrich and members of the Kendall family. Under their direction, *Monteigne* will continue to be a monument to the epic era when cotton was king and the gracious way of life was enjoyed in the South before the Civil War.

PLATE XLI *MONTEIGNE*

Monteigne — Entrance hall
with marble floors.

Drawing room at Monteigne.

Bedroom at Monteigne.

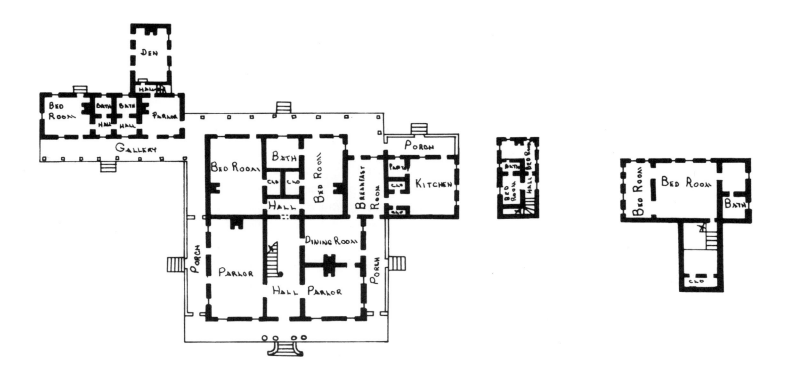

GRIFFITH-MC COMAS HOUSE

Circa 1796

The lot that this early house stands upon was granted to Mr. Hugh Coyle in 1796 by the Spanish Government. In 1799 the property was sold to Mr. Leonard Pomet, who must have built on to the original house and in so doing, enlarged this residence. Mr. Pomet was one of the early merchants who operated a business establishment in Natchez. The property again changed hands with the sale to Reverend Daniel Smith. Reverend Smith made a lasting contribution to Natchez for it was he who formally organized the First Presbyterian Church in this city in 1817. Among other owners who made their imprint in the history of the City of Natchez and the State of Mississippi were Messrs. John and William B. Griffith who founded the Mississippi State Bar Association.

If it had not been for the widow of William B. Griffith, the great naturalist, John James Audubon, may not have painted the beautiful panoramic view of the city of Natchez. Mrs. Griffith had commissioned Mr. Audubon to paint this scene for her, but by the time it was completed, Mrs. Griffith had died. Her heirs refused to accept this painting. Mr. Audubon attempted to sell this work, but could not find a prospective buyer. Finally he deposited it with a storekeeper before moving away from Natchez. This painting was taken to France and then returned to the United States. Today this painting hangs over the mantel in the dining room of Melrose.

Mrs. Ann Willis McComas, who resided here in 1855, was the wife of General Josiah Hillen McComas, who was in command of the local unit of the State Militia which was the official welcoming body that honored Marquis De Lafayette upon his visit to this city in 1825.

The *Griffith-McComas House* was used as a parsonage for the Wall Street Baptist Church and then it was turned into a boarding house. While it was used for that purpose, many partitions were put up and the porches were converted into rooms.

A new future was being planned for the *Griffith-McComas House* in 1960, for it was in this year that Mr. and Mrs. Harold Leisure, formerly of New Orleans, Louisiana, purchased the property. After a careful study of the originial architectural design of the house, a restoration plan was drawn. After a year spent removing unsightly additions and repairing damage which had been inflicted over the years, the house was returned to its original appearance which is a modified example of West Indies design. In the meticulous replacement of the attractive colonettes along the upper and lower porches, which run the width of the house, and the exposure of the lovely fanlighted doorway, this house gives the visitor a realistic view of what one of the early houses located in the Old Spanish section of the city looked like in its prime.

Mrs. Leisure has a most interesting collection of china and silver which consists mainly of very early patterns. Many pieces of this collection have come from the various historic houses of Mississippi and Louisiana. Some of the silver was made by a local silversmith in the early 1800's.

The walls are adorned with rare prints and other objects of art as well as book cases filled with volumes of Southern Americana.

Mr. and Mrs. Leisure operate a rare bookshop in the lower floor of this building. The entire upper floor consists of most attractive living quarters. The Leisures deserve much credit for this historic preservation of a lovely old house which is very much a part of not only the heritage of Natchez but also that of the lower Mississippi Valley.

PLATE XLII *GRIFFITH-MC COMAS HOUSE*

Library at the Griffith-McComas House.

Parlor at the Griffith-McComas House.

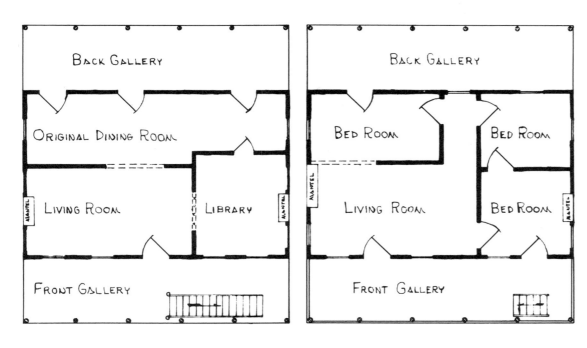

BACK GALLERY

ORIGINAL DINING ROOM

LIVING ROOM

LIBRARY

FRONT GALLERY

FIRST FLOOR PLAN

BACK GALLERY

BED ROOM

BED ROOM

LIVING ROOM

BED ROOM

FRONT GALLERY

SECOND FLOOR PLAN

169

HOMEWOOD

1855-1962

The present house, *Homewood*, was the dependency to the palatial mansion which was destroyed by fire in 1940. This building was one of the most impressive in Natchez. With the labor of scores of slaves, construction was started in 1855 and continued for a period of five years, being completed in 1860. Within the thick walls of this house went one million brick which were burned on the place. Prior to the fire, *Homewood* took its place proudly among the fine residences of the South.

Homewood was built by Mr. David Hunt for his daughter, Catherine, after her marriage to Mr. William Balfour. Mr. Hunt had built another home in 1853, Lansdowne, for his daughter, Charlotte, upon her marriage to Mr. George Marshall, Sr. Lansdowne is a short distance from *Homewood*.

The Balfour family retained possession of *Homewood* through the tragic years of the Civil War and Reconstruction and finally sold the property in 1907 to Mr. William Joseph Kaiser. The Kaiser family occupied *Homewood* until Mrs. Kingsley Swan, a New Yorker, purchased the property in 1937. Mr. and Mrs. Swan completely restored the house and landscaped its grounds. It was during the residency of the Swans that the fire of unknown origin destroyed this lovely house.

After the fire, a lengthy legal battle erupted between the attorneys representing the insurance firm who had written coverage on the house and its contents and the attorneys representing the Swans. This court case was the height of interest in Natchez in 1940. Local residents and newspaper correspondents filled the court room to its fullest. In recent times there had been no other court trial in Natchez that reached the magnitude of this case. Today local residents will tell freely what was said by the two opposing forces prior to the court's decision. After the settlement, Mr. and Mrs. Swan turned and left the towering and forlorn ruins of *Homewood* and Natchez, never to return.

In 1941, Mr. Alvin Laub purchased the land and what was left of this once beautiful estate from the Swans.

Fearing that someone might be injured by falling objects from the ruins, he had the walls pushed down and gave the lovely wrought iron trim to the war cause. After a series of tenants, the one remaining original building fell into despair and needed a complete restoration.

Once again a father gave this property as a gift to his daughter, Mrs. J. Wesley Cooper. In 1962, Mr. and Mrs. Cooper undertook the task of restoring the remaining dependency. This building originally contained three rooms on each floor. The lower floor had been altered in a way to create a triple garage, as shown in the photograph taken before the recent restoration. One room remained undisturbed on the lower floor. This room had been used as a kitchen. The three rooms located on the second floor were used as bedrooms.

When work was started, with a crew of workmen and Mr. Cooper, the entire roof was replaced and all plaster on the interior walls and ceilings was removed. The walls throughout the house were replastered and have a smooth white finish. The garage section was transformed into a larger parlor, and the old kitchen into a dining room. The second floor was redesigned so that it consists of two bedrooms, two baths and a dressing room with walk-in closets. For the necessity of comfortable living, a wing was constructed at each side of the building. The wing to the left contains a spacious kitchen, and behind this, a den. The wing to the right contains a library, bath and master bedroom. The two wings were built with bricks that were dug out of the ruins of the larger house. The floors of the left wing, dining room and parlor are paved with the same old type brick that was used in the walls.

Mr. and Mrs. Cooper are collecting period pieces of furniture and placing them among the family heirlooms throughout the house. Hanging on the walls are many rare documents related to the early history of the South.

With a systemized pattern, the grounds are being restored to their former beauty. There is only a trace of the ruins of the manor house and this too will be gone, for the remnants of this monument to a lush and romantic era which was lost must make room for its counterpart.

PLATE XLIII *HOMEWOOD*

Den located in left wing at Homewood.

Kitchen located in left wing at Homewood.

Homewood as it appeared before restoration.

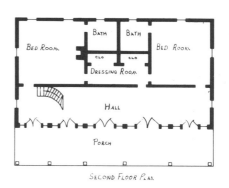

SECOND FLOOR PLAN

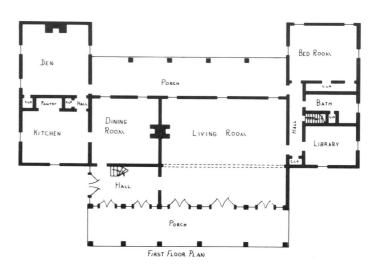

FIRST FLOOR PLAN

SPRINGFIELD

About 1790

Springfield was built 17 miles from Natchez about 1790 by Thomas Marston Green, who served as colonel under General Andrew Jackson. Green had journeyed from Virginia to Natchez, and had arrived during the rule of the Spanish. The house is a two-storied brick house with wide double galleries across the entire front. The galleries are supported by six Doric columns, and the house has the look of an early Spanish plantation house. The upper gallery has hand-made rails.

The brick for *Springfield* was burned on the grounds from native clay. The walls are two feet thick, and the doors half-a-foot thick, for *Springfield* alone in the vicinity of Cole's Creek, was a veritable fortification.

The interior plan is the usual one of the times with the wide central hall flanked by two large rooms and one small on either side. The unusually large mantels were carved by the Spanish workmen. The woodwork is embellished with a hand-carved lace design. At the present time, *Springfield* is not occupied. The current owners are Mr. James H. Williams, Jr. and the heirs of William P. Williams, of St. Louis, Missouri.

A marker on the highway announces this:

SPRINGFIELD

South ¼ miles is the site of mansion. Built by Thos. M. Green, wealthy planter and prominent in public affairs. Here in 1791, Andrew Jackson was married to Rachel Robards.

This was one president of the United States who knew Natchez well. He once lived not far from Natchez, and some say, engaged in slave trade here. But in connection with the lovely home of *Springfield*, he is best known for his tragic romance with beautiful Rachel Robards, for it was at *Springfield* that the two were married.

Through business connections, Andrew Jackson became very close friends with the owner of *Springfield*. It will be recalled that Rachel Robards, who was to become Andrew Jackson's wife and the one love of his life, was separated from her jealous first husband, and journeyed to Natchez to visit the Greens and to recuperate from the trials of her early marriage.

After spending 15 months here and believing herself divorced, she wed Andrew Jackson in a ceremony performed by Mr. Green himself, and spent the first week of her married life at *Springfield*. Later she went with Mr. Jackson to his cottage on Bayou Pierre.

The tragic sequence to this marriage is, of course, history. Robards had never published the divorce decree, and, according to the law of the time, the divorce was not legal. Andrew Jackson and the lovely Rachel had another marriage ceremony performed in 1794; but the young woman became the target for a great deal of talk and later died, broken-hearted, before Andrew Jackson arrived at the National Capitol.

Thus, this beautiful old home, surrounded by trees that were planted by the first owner, remains among the famous landmarks of Mississippi long after Rachel and Andrew Jackson are both gone, to become a link in the history of the presidents of the United States.

Recently, *Springfield* was offered as a gift to the United States Department of the Interior to be incorporated into The Natchez Trace Parkway. The owner, Mr. Williams, his knowledge of the value of this historical house and through his generosity, has made this gesture. It is the hope of the author as well as many of the other historically-minded citizens that the final acceptance of *Springfield* by the National Park Service will be forthcoming.

PLATE XLIV *SPRINGFIELD*

WINDY HILL MANOR

Circa 1787

Windy Hill Manor was one of the most historic houses in the Natchez District. It was here that the ex-Vice President of the United States, Aaron Burr, was a house guest while awaiting his trial for treason against the United States. The owner of *Windy Hill Manor* was Colonel Benjamin Osmun, Aaron Burr's loyal friend. Colonel Osmun extended the invitation to Burr after he was released on a $5000.00 bail.

While Burr was enjoying the hospitality at *Windy Hill*, he met the charming Madeline Price (The Lovely "Maid of Half-way Hill"). Burr wooed Madeline while awaiting his fate. Despite the position menacing him, his attentions to Madeline were not disturbed until he found that he would be hung by a mob. After canvassing his precarious position with Colonel Osmun and several other confederates, he slipped out of *Windy Hill Manor* one stormy night in 1807 and forfeited his bond, never to return to his beloved Madeline or to this region.

In 1818, *Windy Hill Manor* was purchased from the Osmun estate by Colonel Gerard C. Brandon. This was a bridal gift to his daughter, Elizabeth, upon her marriage to William Stanton. Thus *Windy Hill Manor* came under the rule of the Stantons. With the new owners, gaiety filled the rooms of *Windy Hill* again. Many years passed with elaborate evening parties which some said were the most enjoyable they could recall. Then came death to the last male Stanton of *Windy Hill*. A gradual decline set in as the only ones left to maintain the affairs of the plantation were three maiden sisters, Miss Maude, Miss Elizabeth and Miss Beatrice. Deterioration began on the house and outer buildings. Slowly the rear portion of the house rotted away. The sisters worked as hard as they could to maintain a scant livelihood. As the years

passed conditions worsened. With pride, and in poverty, they struggled to hold on to their inheritance, never giving up by forfeiting any of their treasured heirlooms or land, both of which meant so much to them.

A few years ago, the remains of *Windy Hill* were dismantled by a local cabinetmaker. With the loss of this house some of the romance of our country's history has been erased.

Stairway that was at Windy Hill Manor.
COURTESY MR. FRANK PARSONS

Front view of Windy Hill Manor shortly before it was dismantled.

Rear view of Windy Hill Manor as it appeared in 1936.

TEXADA TAVERN

Circa 1790

Texada Tavern was built for Governor Carlos de Grand-Pre and was used as the Spanish Government House. This building has been referred to as the Cabildo for this territory which was under the rule of the Spanish Crown. It was a favorite gathering place for Spanish officials. All of the surrounding town lots were granted to people who were in the good graces of the Spanish Government.

In 1799, Don Manuel Garcia de Tejada purchased the lot and building on the corner of Wall and Washington Streets, after having come to the Natchez Territory from Spain. Note the spelling of the name. *"Tejada"* was the way it was said to have been spelled on early papers in possession of the Texada Family. After acquiring wealth from business enterprises in the sinful Natchez-Under-the-Hill and from several plantations, Mr. Texada purchased this building and it is thought, enlarged it to its present size. For a time, he operated a tavern and inn here.

In 1817, the Mississippi Territorial Legislature met here to organize the State Government. In December of that year some of the most noted personalities in the territory were visitors to this early building.

For many years, *Texada Tavern* was used as a tenement and also as a rooming house. With the lack of interest, the entire building fell into despair, became a large gray eyesore among buildings surrounding it that had been beautifully restored.

In 1964, Dr. and Mrs. George Moss purchased the property and restored a charming dependency located to the rear of *Texada*. This building was originally used as a kitchen and servants' quarters. With this building restored, it has enabled the Mosses to oversee the restoration of the main building. Soon this building that is one of the earliest standing in the Old Spanish Section of the City will become a reminder of the days when the Spanish Dons brought prosperity to Natchez.

The once gray stucco that covered its exterior walls was removed and the natural color of the bricks has been returned. In the panoramic painting of the City of Natchez executed by John James Audubon, it shows *Texada* as being a brick building. The stucco was applied in more recent years to stop further deterioration of the exterior walls.

Texada as it appeared in 1936.
COURTESY MR. FRANK PARSONS

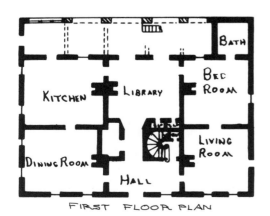

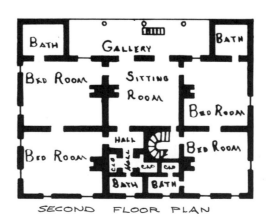

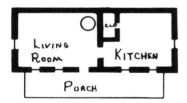

FIRST FLOOR PLAN

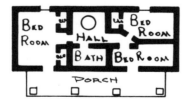

SECOND FLOOR PLAN

NATCHEZ ADAMS COUNTY CHAMBER of COMMERCE

1826

This charming small house located near several of the larger mansions has been described by a member of The American Institute of Architects as one of the best examples of a small town house of its period to be found in Natchez.

It is believed that this house was built for James C. Wilkins by the firm known as Neibert and Gimmell in 1826. Neibert and Gimmell designed and built some of the finest mansions in the Natchez region.

Through the years this house changed hands many times. One owner was not satisfied with his deed to the lot and employed a local legal firm to research the records of ownership. There was a question of the validity of his deed. This lot was the first town lot legalized by a President of the United States in this part of the country. James C. Wilkins deposited a letter with the General Land Office in 1820, but the seal of that Office and the signature of President John Quincy Adams was not affixed until 1825.

With the restoration of this house, one more of the fine houses of Natchez has been saved for future generations to appreciate.

NATCHEZ ADAMS COUNTY CHAMBER of COMMERCE

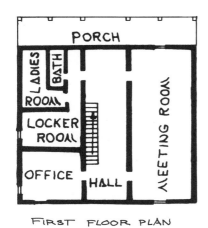

FIRST FLOOR PLAN

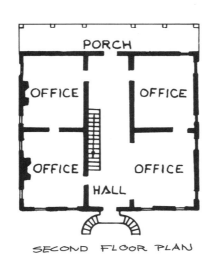

SECOND FLOOR PLAN

TRINITY EPISCOPAL DAY SCHOOL

(Magnolia Hall)

Circa 1858

Magnolia Hall was built by Thomas Henderson in 1858 for his residence. During the Civil War, Natchez was shelled by Union gunboats. A shell hit this fine building and tore through its thick brick walls, exploding in what was the servants' dining hall. Fortunately there were no injuries as the servants had just withdrawn from this room. After Natchez was occupied by Union forces, the Henderson family was ordered to vacate the first floor of their home. The Union command did give them twelve hours to move into the upstairs. Union officers were quartered within the first floor.

Magnolia Hall passed from the Hendersons to the Britton and then the Wheeler families. In later years, the property was purchased by the Armstrongs and operated as a hotel. In 1963, the *Trinity Episcopal Church* purchased the property and converted it into one of the most fashionable schools in this region. The first floor consists of offices on the left and behind that, a massive music room. To the right of the hall, classrooms occupy what was the double drawing rooms. The upper floor consists of four classrooms as well as the two storied ell which also includes the library and cafeteria. Once again the rooms of *Magnolia Hall* ring with the laughter of children.

TRINITY EPISCOPAL DAY SCHOOL

KING'S TAVERN

Circa 1770

King's Tavern is the oldest house in Natchez, and possibly one of the oldest in the Lower Mississippi Valley. It is certainly one of the most fascinating.

Built of ship timber, cypress and brick, its structure is primitive, but tremendously solid. It resembles the block houses of early America, fortified against unfriendly Indians. Its timbers were hewn to size and fitted together with pegs, and in its basement this type of construction can be examined.

When it was built, the present City of Natchez, except for one or two buildings, was probably woods. The main settlements were at Natchez-Under-the-Hill.

The building sits directly on the street. Its base is a brick wall topped by a picket fence on one portion and the wooden structure of the house itself on the other. There is a gallery behind the picket fence, and from the gallery one enters what is now the parlor. This has a fireplace, once very wide, but now filled with an imported grate. All the rooms have low ceilings; and there is indication that *King's Tavern* predates the Spanish period in Natchez, and was probably erected when the English had control of this section.

The basement is one of the most intriguing parts of the house. In one room, which was the tavern kitchen, a fireplace with spit and crane, and a brick oven comprised a large part of the room. One crane is still in the fireplace.

It was also in the basement that the guests were served at a long counter and it takes little imagination to visualize the scene of 180 years ago against such a picturesque background. This room opens onto the sidewalk. Evidently, this opening was the main entrance.

That this building was already standing in 1789 is evidenced by a deed to Richard King dated in that year by the Spanish, which gives this property and buildings to King, an early settler.

In 1823, *King's Tavern* was the home of the Postlethwaites, a very prominent family in Mississippi, whose descendants still live in Natchez. A member of this family stills owns the Tavern.

King's Tavern has been mentioned time and again in early American writings. Delivery of the first United States mail in this area was made from *King's Tavern*, after being brought here by an Indian runner.

An early settler who came to Natchez in 1788 refers to this house in his later memoirs. It has figured in many legends and many stories handed down by word of mouth; and while hearing these stories, one can also see bullet holes in the main doorway, the result of an attack by Indians long ago.

King's Tavern is undergoing an extensive restoration under the direction of its present owners, Mr. and Mrs. W. W. Maxie. Thus this historic and interesting old building is being saved for future generations so that they may gain some idea of how the early settlers lived in the wilderness.

KING'S TAVERN

BRANDON HALL

1855

Brandon Hall is one of the few remaining houses adjacent to the Natchez Trace, from which one enters through a winding wooded road. *Brandon Hall* was built for Gerard Brandon III upon land given to his wife by her father. With the use of slave labor and timbers that were cut from local forests, the house was completed in 1856. This house possesses a different architectural design from others found in this region. One of the unusual features of this house is the arrangement of its porches. The lower porch extends across the front and sides while the upper porch extends only the width of the house; thus, giving the appearance of a double decked steamboat. Whether this achievement was intended by the builder is not known. The interior of *Brandon Hall* is spacious having high ceilings and windows that extend from the floor to the ceilings. A wide entrance hall runs the length of the house with three rooms to each side. To the rear of this hall is a carved staircase that leads to the second floor.

The room arrangement there is a duplication of the first floor.

Sorrow was cast over *Brandon Hall* by the loss of seven of the Brandon children within a period of six years.

For many years, the Brandon Family retained possession of *Brandon Hall*. In 1947, Mr. and Mrs. L. A. White purchased the property and made many needed repairs. After some twenty years of residing here, Mr. and Mrs. White exchanged this house for one located within the City of Natchez. Dr. Harold C. Hawkins and Mr. H. Hal Garner vacated The Wigwam and moved their furnishings to *Brandon Hall*. With the talents that Dr. Hawkins and Mr. Garner possess, it is hoped that they will accomplish the same superb renovation that they attained at The Wigwam.

Under the new owners the grounds are being planted with a variety of native plants, and within a short time will be transformed into their former beauty.

BRANDON HALL

JEFFERSON MILITARY COLLEGE

1802

Jefferson Military College is the oldest endowed college in the Southwestern United States. It was established by an Act of the Legislature of the Mississippi Territory, May 13, 1802, the same year that the United States Military Academy was established at West Point.

The territorial capital had just been moved from Natchez to Washington, then a famous health resort near Natchez, and later *Jefferson Military College* was also established here.

The first president of the College was W. C. C. Claiborne, territorial governor of Mississippi and a friend of President Thomas Jefferson, for whom the College was named. The College was chartered as non-sectarian.

The early years of *Jefferson Military College* were marked by financial problems. The College had little money, and even a lottery planned to raise funds was unsuccessful. Citizens gave it gifts of land, and United States Congress gave it land grants, one of which was later located on the Tombigbee River near the Alabama border.

Finally in October, 1841, a severe blow was suffered when the main building burned. Not only was the property loss excessive, but about 500 valuable volumes in the library, as well as many archives of the Territory of Mississippi, were lost.

The sturdy brick walls of the main building remained, and using this as a base, the trustees raised the structure again. This building still stands, a part of the present-day campus of *Jefferson Military College.*

The campus sits on one hundred acres, and has three modern dormitories. The other five of its buildings are more than a hundred years old. Tremendous oaks shade and mellow the campus, which is one of the historic spots of Mississippi.

Under these great oaks, Aaron Burr was given his preliminary hearing in the great conspiracy trial of 1807. Under these same oaks, the Convention of 1817 drafted the Mississippi Constitution by which Mississippi was admitted as a state into the Union on December 10, 1817.

The College has been through six wars, and during the Civil War was used by the Federal Army as headquarters. Although the early records of the College were lost in the fire, and many of the names of early graduates are unknown, it is known that Jefferson Davis, president of the Confederacy, attended this College before going to West Point, and that John James Audubon, the famous painter and naturalist, was a drawing master here.

Among visitors to the campus were General Andrew Jackson and his troops, who camped under the oaks in 1815 before marching back to Tennessee after the Battle of New Orleans. General Lafayette visited the College in 1825 and reviewed a drill by the cadets. After 160 years, cadets in their trim uniforms marched at review at *Jefferson Military College.* The lack of funds forced the College to suspend classes in 1964. This, one of the most historic spots in Mississippi, is slumbering to deterioration. What a shame to lose such a landmark.

JEFFERSON MILITARY COLLEGE

NATCHEZ TRACE

Of all the beauties of Natchez, the most ancient is not a house nor a building, but a peaceful trail sunken deep in spots beneath the level of the terrain, overshadowed by trees and mosses and vines.

This is the *Natchez Trace,* the 500-mile roadway from Nashville, Tennessee, to Natchez, through whose hazardous route the early settlers from the East came to Natchez. *The Trace* evolved with the development of the country.

The Trace was here long before Columbus set sail to find a short route to India. Hooves of wild buffalos and other animals beat it out as the best path through the woods, skirting gaunt hills and deep morrasses. Indians on the hunt followed the animal path and marked it, as was their custom. It was a bare foot path, a trail hardly discernible; but when Natchez and the Southwest were being settled, the Eastern men and women found it, followed it, and through the years, it became something of a roadway.

The history of the *Natchez Trace* is completely tied up with the history of Natchez and Texas. The earliest explorers and settlers probably came down by way of the Mississippi River, but were unable to return by this means because of the heavy currents in the river. This was the day of the flatboat, and long before the steamboat era. The boatmen sold their boats and freight in Natchez, and made the trip back by foot overland by way of the *Natchez Trace.*

It was the most primitive of roadways. As the years passed, adventurers and even entire families, came down *The Trace*. The travelers were required to sleep out of doors. At first the trail was so narrow that even wagons could not travel on it so that men used horses or walked. Rough little inns grew up at long intervals along the highway.

There were many dangers — exposure to the elements, disease, Indians and murderous highwaymen. Hundreds who started on the trip were never heard of again. Yet, knowing all these hazards, men and women continued to journey to the newer land, and it was their feet that beat the path into a roadway.

By Act of the Federal Congress in 1938, the *Natchez Trace Parkway* was made a project of the National Park Service, and is being restored as one of the historic monuments of this country. It will connect with other scenic highways, to become a primary tourist attraction.

Modern engineering has caused shorter roadways to be constructed, and until restoration began, a part of the *Trace* was lost from lack of use.

It is a beautiful highway. Characteristics of the soil around Natchez have caused the highway to sink far below the level of the surrounding ground by constant use, so that the road is like a tunnel in spots. The trees above the road are old, and hung with moss and vines. In the photograph shown here, vines and trees have joined over the road, making a picturesque natural tunnel.

NATCHEZ TRACE

Steamboat docked at the Natchez wharf about 1880.
FROM THE BLANKENSTEIN COLLECTION

NATCHEZ UPON THE HILL.

Natchez-Upon-the-Hill in 1865 from an old wood cut.

COURTESY THE NATCHEZ GARDEN CLUB

Franklin Street, the 500 block, from Locust Street
looking east, December 1889. Building to the right
houses Pyron Furniture Company.
COURTESY THE LATE MISS EVADNE BEEKMAN

Silver Street — part of the notorious Natchez-Under-
the-Hill as it appeared in 1875.
FROM THE BLANKENSTEIN COLLECTION

The South side of Main Street in the 400 block, as it appeared about 1900.
FROM THE BLANKENSTEIN COLLECTION

Natchez-Under-the-Hill in 1876, looking south.
COURTESY MISS DIANNE BAKER

State Street between Pearl and Wall Streets, looking west.
COURTESY MR. N. LESLIE CARPENTER

Masonic Temple located on the northwest
corner of Main Street at the intersection of
Union Street, as it appeared in about 1865.
This building was demolished to make way
for the Masonic Temple Opera House.
COURTESY THE LATE MRS. B. R. MODESITT

The Natchez Water Front in 1885.
COURTESY MRS. JEANERETTE HARLOW

West side of Commerce Street, corner of Franklin, as it appeared in about 1885.
FROM THE AUTHOR'S COLLECTION

Commerce Street at the intersection of Franklin Street,
looking south. This building housed one of the early news-
papers of Natchez, The Natchez Sun.
Photographed about 1885.

FROM THE BLANKENSTEIN COLLECTION

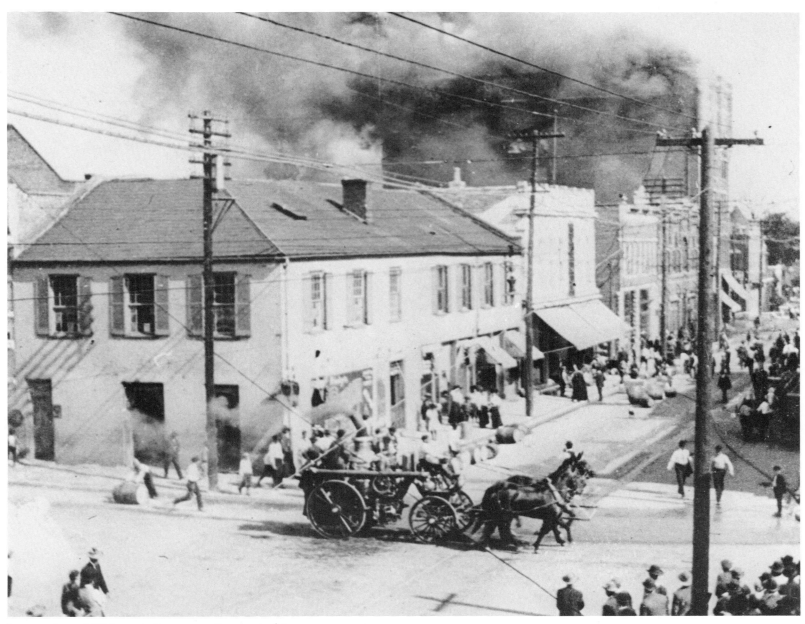

Intersection of Main and Commerce Streets, looking east. Building on fire is the Masonic Temple Opera House shortly after an explosion which destroyed the entire structure in 1908. Note horse-drawn fire engine and man rolling a barrel of whiskey out of corner building.

PHOTOGRAPHED BY THE LATE MR. PAUL R. SIMMONS

Main Street in the 500 block as it appeared
in 1890, looking west.
FROM THE BLANKENSTEIN COLLECTION

River Front at Natchez
as it appeared before 1885.
Note steamboats docked at
the foot of Silver Street.
FROM THE BLANKENSTEIN COLLECTION

South Commerce Street at the intersection of Washington Street. Buildings to the right are the Trinity Episcopal Church and the Temple B'nai Israel. Photograph taken in the Spring of 1905.

FROM THE BLANKENSTEIN COLLECTION

Southwest section of Natchez as it appeared about 1880.
Steeple in center of photograph is the First Presbyterian
Church. Dome to the right is the Adams County Court
House.

Union Street looking north at the intersection of Franklin.
Note Jefferson Hotel. Extreme left can be seen Stanton
Hall, to the right, Jefferson Street Methodist Church.
Photographed in the 1880's.
FROM THE BLANKENSTEIN COLLECTION

South Central section of Natchez as it appeared in 1905.
FROM THE BLANKENSTEIN COLLECTION

Part of Natchez-Under-the-Hill as it appeared in the 1880's. Today most of this section has been taken by the river.

FROM THE BLANKENSTEIN COLLECTION

Rankin Street looking north from Franklin Street. The two large buildings in the background are St. Mary's Orphanage as they appeared in the early 1900's.

FROM THE BLANKENSTEIN COLLECTION

Silver Street looking north, as it appeared about 1867,
shortly after a storm had hit Natchez.
FROM THE AUTHOR'S COLLECTION

Water Front at Natchez in 1890. Note steamboat, The
Natchez, docked at the wharf.
FROM THE BLANKENSTEIN COLLECTION

TOPICAL INDEX